My Nuclear Nightmare

My Nuclear Nightmare

Leading Japan through the Fukushima Disaster to a Nuclear-Free Future

Naoto Kan

Translated from the Japanese
by Jeffrey S. Irish

Cornell University Press

Ithaca and London

東電福島原発事故 総理大臣として考えたこと
"TOUDEN FUKUSHIMA GENPATSU JIKO SOURIDAIJIN TO SHITE
KANGAETA KOTO"

Copyright 2012 by Naoto Kan

Original Japanese edition published by Gentosha Inc., Tokyo, Japan
English edition is published by arrangement with Gentosha Inc., Tokyo,
Japan, through Discover 21, Inc., Tokyo, Japan

First published 2017 by Cornell University Press

Printed in the United States of America

Library of Congress Cataloging-in-Publication Data

Names: Kan, Naoto, 1946– author.
Title: My nuclear nightmare : leading Japan through the Fukushima
    disaster to a nuclear-free future / Naoto Kan ; translated from
    the Japanese by Jeffrey S. Irish.
Other titles: Touden Fukushima Genpatsu Jiko. English
Description: Ithaca ; London : Cornell University Press, 2017. | Includes
    bibliographical references and index.
Identifiers: LCCN 2016036882 | ISBN 9781501705816 (cloth : alk. paper) |
    ISBN 9781501706660 (epub/mobi) | ISBN 9781501706110 (pdf)
Subjects: LCSH: Fukushima Nuclear Disaster, Japan, 2011. | Nuclear power
    plants—Accidents—Japan | Nuclear energy—Government policy—Japan.
Classification: LCC TK1365.J3 K35613 2017 | DDC 363.17/990952117—dc23
LC record available at https://lccn.loc.gov/2016036882

Cornell University Press strives to use environmentally responsible
suppliers and materials to the fullest extent possible in the publishing
of its books. Such materials include vegetable-based, low-VOC inks
and acid-free papers that are recycled, totally chlorine-free, or partly
composed of nonwood fibers. For further information, visit our website
at www.cornellpress.cornell.edu.

Cloth printing   10 9 8 7 6 5 4 3 2 1

Contents

Preface to the English Translation

Five years after the accident at the Fukushima Daiichi Nuclear Power Plant, I am pleased to finally share with the English-speaking world the realities of this nuclear nightmare.

While we are powerless to stop earthquakes, tsunamis, and other natural disasters, this is not true of nuclear disasters. If we shut down and dismantle all our nuclear power plants, we will no longer have nuclear accidents. With the hope that we will rid the world of nuclear power facilities as soon as possible, I dedicate this translation to the victims of the many nuclear accidents our world has known.

Preface to the Japanese Edition

I served as prime minister of Japan for the 452 days from June 8, 2010, until September 2, 2011. It goes without saying that the most significant events during my tenure were the Great East Japan earthquake and the accident at Tokyo Electric Power Company's Fukushima Daiichi Nuclear Power Plant that followed. From the moment I relinquished my role as prime minister, I began to think about the need to leave behind some form of record of those events.

Now that the report by the National Diet of Japan Fukushima Nuclear Accident Independent Investigation Commission and other research reports have been made public, and before my memory fades, I have chosen to take pen in hand. I would like to clarify what I know as precisely as possible. Then, beyond merely reviewing the facts, I would like to share the thoughts I had as I made the decisions I made, and how I felt as I took various actions as prime minister in the vortex of a nuclear accident.

The evaluation of a politician's actions, of his or her work, is not up to the politician. While I feel that I acted selflessly and put my life on the line, it is not my place to judge. Ultimately the evaluation of my actions must be entrusted to history. However, as the prime minister who did everything in his power to guide Japan through its nuclear nightmare, I *can* make this judgment: Japan must put an end to the use of nuclear power.

Timeline for Nuclear Power and the Fukushima Accident

June 27, 1954	First nuclear power plant to be connected to an external grid goes operational in Obninsk, outside of Moscow
July 25, 1966	Japan begins commercial use of nuclear power–generated electricity
March 28, 1979	Accident at Three Mile Island nuclear power plant
April 26, 1986	Accident at nuclear power plant in Chernobyl
June 8, 2010	Naoto Kan becomes prime minister
March 11, 2011	9.0 magnitude earthquake and tsunami strike northeast Japan, accident at Fukushima Daiichi Nuclear Power Plant begins to unfold, evacuation of area around plant commences
March 12	PM Kan visits Fukushima by helicopter, hydrogen explosion at Fukushima's Unit 1 reactor
March 13	Meltdown at Fukushima's Unit 3 reactor
March 14	Hydrogen explosion at Fukushima's Unit 3 reactor

March 15	PM Kan addresses employees at Tokyo Electric Power Company, PM Kan establishes Government-TEPCO Integrated Response Office (IRO)
March 16	Self-Defense Forces helicopter unable to drop water on the reactors due to high radiation, PM Kan talks with UN secretary general Ban Ki-moon
March 17	SDF helicopters succeed in pouring water on reactors
April 2	Discovery of water contaminated with radioactive substances flowing from Fukushima Daiichi into the Pacific Ocean
April 17	TEPCO releases "A Roadmap for the Containment of the Accident at the Fukushima Daiichi Nuclear Power Plant"
May 6	PM Kan requests shutdown of Hamaoka Nuclear Power Plant
May 10	PM Kan announces preparations for the establishment of a nuclear accident investigation committee
May 24	Nuclear accident investigation committee approved by Kan's cabinet
June 2	Kan cabinet no-confidence motion submitted to the Diet, PM Kan promises to resign after several goals are achieved
July 13	PM Kan publicly declares resolve to "strive for a society free of dependence on nuclear power"
August 26	Bill to promote renewable energy passes
September 2	Naoto Kan resigns and is replaced by Yoshihiko Noda

May 2012	All of Japan's nuclear reactors are off-line
September 2012	Noda administration commits to total elimination of nuclear power by the 2030s
December 2012	Liberal Democratic Party (LDP) returns to power, with Shinzo Abe as prime minister
August 2015	First nuclear reactor goes back online, in Kagoshima, Japan

My Nuclear Nightmare

Prologue

MY NUCLEAR NIGHTMARE

I often recall the harsh conditions of that first week. From the time of the earthquake disaster on March 11, 2011, I stayed in the prime minister's office complex and, when I was alone, napped in my disaster fatigues on a couch in the reception room located behind the office where I conducted my official duties. When I say that I "napped," I was really just lying down and resting my body while my mind raced, thinking frantically about how to cope with the earthquake and tsunami, about the potential escalation of the nuclear accident, and whether it could be contained. I have no recollection of actually sleeping.

Awakening

I had vivid memories of the Hanshin-Awaji earthquake in 1995. Recalling the importance of a quick response, I hastened to dispatch the Self-Defense Forces. It goes without saying that this was my first direct encounter with a nuclear accident. Having read reports of Chernobyl, I had some sense of the horrors of such an accident, but I could never have imagined that one would occur here in Japan.

The Chernobyl nuclear accident involved an older type graphite-moderated reactor and a series of operational mistakes that led to a runaway nuclear reaction, an explosion, and the release of large quantities of radioactive material. It was my understanding at the time that the accident occurred because the reactor was old and Soviet technology was inadequate. Because Japan possessed unparalleled nuclear technology and superior experts and engineers, I believed that a Chernobyl-type accident could not occur at a Japanese nuclear power plant. To my great consternation, I would come to learn that this was a safety myth created by Japan's "Nuclear Village" [a vast and powerful network of vested interests].

Prior to March 2011, the largest nuclear accident Japan had experienced was at Tokaimura, in 1999. That accident was caused by careless management by the company handling the nuclear fuel. Two workers died from radiation poisoning. I recall taking an interest in the matter and studying it. I realized that the accident had resulted from human error, but somehow I didn't recognize that human error could lead to a larger nuclear accident. Thinking back on it now, I regret that I had not learned that people do make mistakes, and with that in mind, we needed to be prepared for a nuclear accident.

Back in my college days, at the Tokyo Institute of Technology, I majored in applied physics. I studied and have an understanding of the fundamentals of nuclear power but have never designed a nuclear reactor, nor am I a specialist in the field. Just the same, I am more acquainted with this area than politicians educated in the liberal arts, and my knowledge did help me understand what was happening at the Fukushima plant.

We received word that immediately after the earthquake, the automatic emergency shutdown apparatus had shut down Fukushima's reactors. I recall being relieved by this news, but later we received a report that when the tsunami struck, all power had failed and the cooling systems were not functioning. This shocked me to the point that my face began to twitch. I knew that if a nuclear reactor was not cooled, even after it had been shut down, a meltdown would occur.

Prior to this accident I had not visited the Fukushima power plants, but immediately afterward I had my executive secretary Kenji Okamoto research the facility. I learned that there were six reactors and seven spent fuel pools at Fukushima's Daiichi [No. 1] Nuclear Power Plant, and four reactors and four spent fuel pools at Fukushima's Daini [No. 2] Nuclear Power Plant, located twelve kilometers [7.5 miles] away. The six reactors at Fukushima Daiichi had a capacity of 4,696 megawatts, and the four reactors at Fukushima Daini a capacity of 4,400 megawatts, for a total of 9,096 megawatts. Chernobyl's four reactors had a total generation capacity of 3,800 megawatts. Fukushima's capacity was 2.4 times as large. And whereas the Chernobyl accident had involved only one reactor, the quantity of nuclear fuel and nuclear waste at the Fukushima plants was dozens of times greater than that.

I was surprised to find such a large concentration of Tokyo Electric Power Company's [hereafter TEPCO's] nuclear power plants located in Fukushima Prefecture. A sense of dread came over me when I thought of what would happen if these plants were disabled. And that is what came to pass.

From Bad to Worse

As an immediate response to the earthquake and tsunami, Ryu Matsumoto, minister of state for disaster management, was stationed at the Crisis Management Center in the basement of the prime minister's office complex. Matsumoto contacted Toshimi

Kitazawa, the minister of defense; Kansei Nakano, the secretary of state (who is also responsible for the police and is chairman of the National Public Safety Commission); and Yoshihiro Katayama, the minister of internal affairs and communications. Before long, these men were all on the move.

While establishing response headquarters for the earthquake and nuclear accident, I worried about the direction the nuclear accident would take for no one had any idea how it would unfold. Normally, even if the power lines stop transmitting electricity, large emergency diesel generators are supposed to supply power. But the tsunami had also knocked out the emergency generators and there was no source of electricity. At the request of TEPCO, we immediately made arrangements for power-supply trucks to supply electricity to the emergency cooling system, but the plugs did not match, and the trucks were ultimately of no use.

I was irritated that the first actions taken in response to the nuclear accident were not accomplished more smoothly. The Nuclear and Industrial Safety Agency [NISA], the government organization that should be at the center of any response to a nuclear accident, offered neither a status update nor a forecast of what lay ahead. I had previously served as minister of health, labor and welfare and as minister of finance, and the bureaucrats at the helm of each of these ministries were experts in their related fields. It was common practice, even before the minister gave any orders, for the bureaucracy to consider a course of action and make a proposal. But the director-general of NISA was not a nuclear energy expert, and his explanation of the situation in Fukushima was inadequate. Moreover, no suggestions were forthcoming with regard to actions that might be taken to address the ongoing crisis.

Shortly after the accident occurred, I had no choice but to devise a means by which the prime minister's office could gather information, with my special advisers and executive secretary at the center of this undertaking.

When the earthquake struck, the control rods that are used to halt the nuclear fission chain reaction were immediately and automatically inserted in the cores of the three reactors that were operating at that time. Although this stopped the chain reactions in each of these reactors, the heat given off by the decay of nuclear fuel makes continuous cooling necessary. Otherwise, the water in the reactors will evaporate, the fuel rods will be exposed, overheat, and ultimately melt down. After an emergency shutdown, cooling has to continue, but in Fukushima's case every electrical source that could have powered the cooling systems had been incapacitated, and the cooling systems ceased to function. This was a grave situation.

In the event of a fire at a thermoelectric power plant, even if the fuel tank were to ignite, the fuel would eventually burn out and the accident would be brought under control. Naturally, the damages would be extensive, but they would be geographically and temporally limited. Depending on how dangerous the situation became, employees might have to be evacuated, and if nothing more could be done, firefighters might be forced to abandon the site.

An accident at a nuclear power plant is fundamentally different. If one leaves an unmanageable nuclear reactor to its own devices, with the passage of time the situation will only grow worse. Once a large quantity of radioactive matter has escaped, workers are unable to approach the site and the situation spirals out of control. This is to say, if one temporarily deserts the site with the intention of regrouping, conditions will only grow all the more dire. The fuel will burn indefinitely, releasing radioactive materials all the while. This radioactive matter will be scattered by the wind, and, to make matters worse, the radiation's toxicity will last for a very long time without dissipating. After all, the half-life of plutonium is 24,000 years.

Four days after the accident, from the night of March 14 through the early dawn hours of March 15, TEPCO entertained the possibility of leaving the site. This would have meant the abandonment of ten nuclear reactors and eleven spent fuel pools and the possibility that Japan would be decimated.

Worst-Case Scenario

During the first week after the nuclear accident, problems steadily escalated. We would later learn that at approximately 7 p.m. on March 11, the day of the earthquake and tsunami, a meltdown had already occurred in the Unit 1 reactor. It had been reported that the fuel remained submerged at that time, but the water gauge was broken. On the afternoon of the twelfth, a hydrogen explosion occurred at the Unit 1 reactor. On March 13, Unit 3 melted down, and on the fourteenth a hydrogen explosion occurred there as well. Then, on March 15, at around 6 a.m., when I was visiting TEPCO's headquarters, there were reports of a crashing sound in Unit 2, and at nearly the same time a hydrogen explosion occurred at Unit 4.

I began to consider just how far this accident might go, and to contemplate a "worst-case scenario." After the initial accident occurred, the United States instructed its citizens to evacuate an area within an eighty-kilometer [fifty-mile] radius of the plant. Many European countries closed their embassies in Tokyo and began to move their employees to the Kansai region, which includes Osaka, Kyoto, and Kobe.

If we lost control of all Fukushima's reactors, over the course of several weeks or months all the reactors and all the spent fuel pools would melt down, and an immense quantity of radioactive material would be released. If this came to pass, the evacuation of a large area, including Tokyo, would be unavoidable. If that became necessary, how could we accomplish an orderly evacuation?

In addition to the evacuation of the general public, we would have to consider moving the Imperial Palace and other state institutions. For several days after the initial accident, when I found myself alone at night, I imagined various evacuation scenarios, but I did not discuss this matter with anyone until the predawn hours of March 15, when I became aware that TEPCO might abandon the site. This situation was so grave I felt I had to use the utmost discretion when putting it into words.

I had been thinking about a worst-case scenario for about a week when, after the successful application of water thanks to the life-threatening efforts of site workers, members of the Self-Defense Forces, firefighters, and others, it appeared that we had begun to extract ourselves from the greatest danger. I think it was around March 22 that, through my special adviser Goshi Hosono, I asked Shunsuke Kondo, the chairman of the Japan Atomic Energy Commission, to conduct a scientific evaluation of the area that would have to be evacuated if everything that could go wrong did go wrong. This is what the Japanese press later referred to as "the prime minister's office's 'worst-case scenario.'" I received the evaluation from Dr. Kondo on March 25. Entitled "A Roughly Sketched Contingency Plan for the Fukushima Daiichi Nuclear Power Plant," it was a highly technical forecast stating that: "If Unit 1's containment vessel is destroyed by a hydrogen explosion, and, due to an increase in the quantity of radioactive material, workers are forced to evacuate the site and are unable to flood and cool units 2 and 3 with water, radioactive material will be discharged by these reactors and by the spent fuel pools in units 1

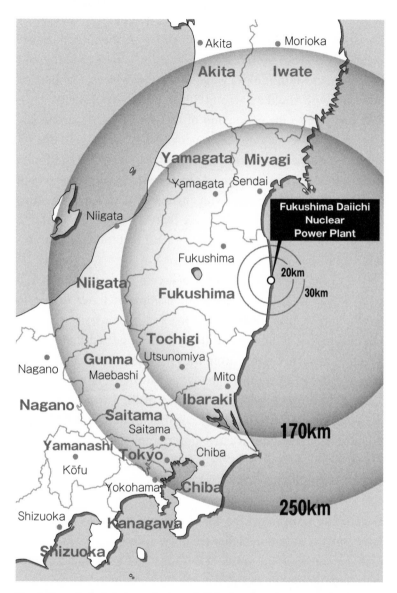

Simulation of a forced evacuation area (170 km) and a voluntary evacuation area (250 km) in the event the accident cannot be contained. Map based on the report of Shunsuke Kondo, chairman of the Japan Atomic Energy Commission, "A Roughly Sketched Contingency Plan for the Fukushima Daiichi Nuclear Power Plant," compiled at the request of the author and dated March 25, 2011.

through 4, and there is the possibility that a forced evacuation would be required for an area within a 170-kilometer [106-mile] radius of the site and a voluntary evacuation area of 250 kilometers [155 miles], including Tokyo."[1]

What I had imagined was now being scientifically substantiated by an expert. Learning that it was true sent a chill down my spine.

To avoid any misunderstanding, in the event of a worst-case scenario, the immediate evacuation of an area with a 250-kilometer radius would not have been required. There would have been several weeks before it was necessary to evacuate Tokyo.

Just the same, a radius of 250 kilometers encompassed all of northeastern Honshu with the exception of Aomori, most of Niigata Prefecture, part of Nagano Prefecture, and most of Kanto, including the Tokyo metropolitan area. Approximately 50 million people live in this area, so 50 million people would have to be evacuated. According to Chairman Kondo's "worst case scenario," with a natural attenuation of radiation levels, it would take several dozen years before people could live in the area again.

The evacuation of 50 million people for several dozen years was on the scale of Sakyo Komatsu's earthquake and tsunami disaster novel, *Japan Sinks* [published in 1973]. There was no precedent we could turn to even abroad. To be sure, this "worst-case scenario" was prepared unofficially, and I did not ask any politicians or government officials to draw up an evacuation plan.

I did, however, privately imagine a scenario involving the evacuation of 50 million people within several weeks. While giving the order to evacuate, we would also have to present an evacuation plan. Without a plan to conform to, total panic would have been inevitable.

In present-day Japan, we do not have martial law,[2] but without the use of state power approaching martial law, an orderly evacuation would not be possible. However, if I had ordered the preparation of an evacuation plan on this scale, it would most certainly have been exposed prior to its execution. Advances in media, in the traditional press and on the Internet, have made it quite difficult to control information. I am not referring to the difficulty of hiding something but the challenge of conveying information precisely, in a manner that would not cause total panic. So, under such conditions, how should one proceed with the evacuation of the Tokyo metropolitan area? Such an operation defies the imagination.

It would probably be necessary to place the trains, roads, and airports under the complete control of the government. Otherwise, systematic movement would be impossible. How should people who are unable to move under their own power—those who are hospitalized or the elderly living in care facilities—how should they be moved and where should they go? Should children and pregnant women be evacuated first? The timing of the evacuation of the imperial family must also be handled with great care. And concurrent with the evacuation of the general public, the removal of government institutions had to be considered as well. For all intents and purposes, this meant the movement of the capital. The central government ministries and agencies, the Diet, and the Supreme Court all had to be moved. A large number of other administrative bodies would also have to be moved outside the 250-kilometer area. In more peaceful times it would take two years, perhaps more, to draw up such plans. But the planning and its implementation had to be accomplished in several weeks.

The Japanese people's composure in response to this earthquake disaster received international praise, but if it had come down to the evacuation of 50 million people in several weeks, I envisioned hell. The lives of 50 million people would have been ruined. *Japan Sinks* would have become a reality.

I want you to try to imagine what you would do if you were ordered to evacuate. This was not like moving; you would basically flee, leaving all your household effects behind. What would you be able to take along? Would you be able to go together, as a family? Where would you go? Those of you with relatives in western Japan might be able to stay with them for a time. But even if you succeeded somehow in evacuating, what would you do about work, housing, and school for your children?

In fact, the approximately 160,000 people who lived near the Fukushima Daiichi Nuclear Power Plant who were evacuated faced these uncertainties. They have suffered greatly. If 50 million people had, in fact, been evacuated, the confusion and adversity that awaited them would have been truly unimaginable. And this was not an idle fantasy. It was so close to becoming a reality.

Even if we were somehow able to evacuate 50 million people, the worst-case scenario would not have stopped there. Imagine people unable to live within a 250-kilometer [155-mile] radius of the plant for dozens of years. Those who had farmed, raised livestock, or fished would lose not only their homes but their livelihoods as well. Those who had worked in factories operated by major corporations might be relocated domestically or even to a location overseas, but locally owned plants would probably go bankrupt, and their workers would find themselves unemployed. The same would be true of privately owned stores. As for department stores, supermarkets, and other distributors, those operating nationwide might be able to avoid bankruptcy, but a reduction in personnel would be inevitable. Companies providing services such as rail, electricity, gas, and communications would lose a substantial volume of work in eastern Japan.

And what about government employees whose jobs would normally be thought of as stable? Those working for the national government would be busy with the major undertaking of rebuilding their country. There might even be a move to increase the number of employees. But what about those who worked for local governments in the 250-kilometer area? While certain villages and towns would continue to exist conceptually, with their residents scattered, they would cease to function as self-governing entities. A minimum number of employees might be stationed at local governments in the surrounding area awaiting the day when they could return home.

A housing allowance would also be needed by evacuees, since the provision of more than 10 million temporary housing units was not a possibility. Even if the government rented and provided rooms in hotels, inns, abandoned homes, and the like, there would be a limit to what we could do.

And what should be done about the more than 10 million people who lost their jobs? Recovery work was not an option because areas damaged by the earthquake and tsunami would have been evacuated and would no longer exist. And what about the schools? Private schools located within the evacuation area would fold. The same would be true of the universities. Even if the students and faculty succeeded in evacuating, there would be no choice but to leave laboratories and other facilities behind. And would there be enough hospitals, clinics, and nursing homes to take in all the sick and elderly?

Even those companies outside the evacuation area, if they were doing business in Tokyo, would not be able to collect any money due and would lose their clients. Whether directly or indirectly, all industries, all businesses would be affected. Financial chaos was inevitable; there would be no alternative but to call a halt to the trading of stocks. The yen would depreciate significantly and the entire Japanese economy would fall into a bottomless pit.

Whereas the price of land in Tokyo would undoubtedly plunge, land prices in Osaka and Nagoya might suddenly rise. It would be necessary to suspend the buying and selling of land. There would be no alternative but to disown the concepts of capitalism and private property. Some people would probably move overseas, much like they did in *Japan Sinks*. How much would the country have to spend? Where would revenues come from?

Conditions requiring the evacuation of a 250-kilometer area would also lead to the global spread of radiation via the atmosphere and ocean currents. How would Japan respond to the ensuing international criticism and the calls for compensation? Placing the blame on TEPCO, a privately owned company, would probably not be acceptable, and costs would already have exceeded TEPCO's capacity to deal with them. This simulation was on a scale far greater than I alone could comprehend.

Images of an impending crisis would not leave my mind. Japanese society had believed that a major accident would not occur at a nuclear power plant, and that premise had been responsible for the construction of fifty-four reactors in Japan. Our laws, our institutions, our government and economy, even our culture had revolved around the conviction that a nuclear accident would not occur. One could say we were totally unprepared, so when an accident actually happened we were unable to handle it. Because we had presumed that a major accident would not occur, there was no system in place for the management of a crisis.

When politicians and electric companies and the responsible ministries say they had not imagined it could happen, they are, in some sense, telling the truth. And they make that assertion while admonishing themselves. But once the accident did occur, regardless of whether it was something we had foreseen or not, there was no running from the fact that it had happened, and I prepared myself accordingly.

The Anguish of Ultimate Responsibility

During the weeks following March 11, 2011, northeastern Japan was occupied by an invisible enemy called radiation. The enemy was not an invader from abroad, and though many may not think of it in this way, it was an enemy that we ourselves had created. Which was all the more reason why we had to contain it ourselves. And in doing so, we had to prepare for the possibility that there would be victims. That is how serious the situation had become.

In the Soviet Union, the military was dispatched in order to contain the Chernobyl nuclear accident, and five thousand tons of sand and lead were dropped from helicopters to extinguish the fire. Then, over the course of the following six months, a stone coffin, a sarcophagus, was built to encase the defective reactor. During the first ten days, in the course of extinguishing the fire, more than two hundred workers, most of them military personnel, were hospitalized. It has been reported that some thirty of them died from acute radiation exposure. When later casualties are taken into account, it is said that a considerable number of soldiers died. It being the Soviet Union, just how many died is unknown, but without a doubt it was desperate, death-defying work. Could Japan respond in a similar fashion? Would it even be permissible?

In Japan, up until the end of the Pacific War, dying for one's country was taken for granted, and those in command, in battles like the one in Okinawa, demanded it not only of soldiers but of the general public as well. After the war, in an act of self-examination, Japan was reborn as a country that would not require this kind of sacrifice. A single human life became heavier than the Earth itself.

But in the face of the nuclear accident in Fukushima, could we take adequate action while protecting this way of thinking? If we failed at containment, and large quantities of radioactive material were discharged throughout northeastern Japan and the rest of the world, what would become of us all? Doubtless, a large number of Japanese would lose their lives, society would descend into chaos, and our very existence as a country would be threatened. Was the fact that lives were at risk an acceptable reason for running away?

In my political principles I have always aspired to the realization of a society with as little unhappiness as possible. While war is the source of the greatest sorrow, a major nuclear accident also brings misery to a large number of people. It is the government's responsibility to curb this misery. And to make this possible, the people must contribute in a manner commensurate with their position in society. Of course, politicians and civil servants bear the greatest responsibility. In the case of the nuclear accident at Fukushima, the employees of TEPCO—the plant's operator—must be prepared to take responsibility as well.

As prime minister, I was required to give orders to go to the site, even though I knew that in the worst case, a person might die. But what of the person who was ordered to go? Some were married and had children; they were caught between their responsibility as a husband and parent not to go to a dangerous place and their responsibility to carry out their work.

During a period of several days beginning on March 11, as we lost control of one reactor after another, I repeatedly asked myself how we could fight against radiation, our invisible enemy, and just how far we could go. We had been driven into a corner, and the corner was right in front of us.

Evacuation

For several days after the initial nuclear accident, the reactors became increasingly difficult to control, and there was no prospect of containment. I decided that we would not run away, even if it meant risking our lives, my own included. Meanwhile, NISA, the administrative body that should have taken the lead in responding to the nuclear accident, made no suggestions, and, beginning a few days after the accident, the director-general rarely showed his face. It was also at this time that TEPCO's intention to withdraw from the site was brought to my attention.

At 3 o'clock on the morning of March 15, when I was trying to get some rest on the couch in the reception room behind my office, I was awakened by my executive secretary with the words "The minister of economy, trade, and industry has arrived and would like to discuss something with you." Then Banri Kaieda, the minister in question, came in and told me that he had received word from TEPCO's president Masataka Shimizu of their intention to desert the site.

I will write in more detail about TEPCO in a future chapter, but my thought at the time was "Abandonment would mean the end of Japan. Abandonment is not an option." That did not apply to TEPCO alone. I felt the same way about the Self-Defense Forces, the fire department, and the police. It could be said that I was demanding too much of a privately owned company, but TEPCO was the party responsible for the accident, and TEPCO's technicians were the only people able to operate the reactors at Fukushima's nuclear power plants. There was no chance of containing the accident without them. Even if it meant risking their lives, I could not allow TEPCO to pull out.

At the same time, I determined the need for a joint command center for the government and TEPCO, located in the company's headquarters. I appointed my special adviser Goshi Hosono as the secretariat in my stead and decided to station him there. In the aftermath of the accident, it was essential for the government and

TEPCO to be united in our efforts to bring the situation under control. But on a vital matter such as the evacuation of the site, our understanding of one another had been inadequate. As we strived to contain the accident, I feared that a misunderstanding might prove fatal, so I asked President Shimizu to visit my office. I told him that desertion was not an option. I also suggested that a joint command center [what would become the Government-TEPCO Integrated Response Office] be placed in TEPCO's headquarters. He agreed.

To lay the groundwork for the establishment of a joint command center, I went to TEPCO's headquarters at 5:35 a.m. on March 15. The idea of abandoning the site was not President Shimizu's alone. The chairman and other TEPCO executives most likely shared his view, so I stood before them and spoke with all my might in the hope that I could convince them not to leave the site:

> More than anyone, you all know the gravity of the situation we are in. There is a need for the government and TEPCO to strategize together, in real time. I will be the director, and Minister Kaieda and President Shimizu will be the deputy directors.
>
> I'm not just concerned about reactor Unit 2. If we abandon reactor Unit 2, what will happen to 1, 3, 4, 5, and 6? And what will happen to Fukushima Daini? If we withdraw, within months all the reactors and nuclear waste will further deteriorate, resulting in the spread of radiation. It would be two or three times the size of Chernobyl, equal to ten or twenty reactors.
>
> Japan will cease to exist if we don't risk our lives to bring this situation under control. We cannot withdraw quietly and watch from afar. If we were to do that, it would not be out of the question for a foreign country to come along and take our place.
>
> You are all party to this, so I ask you to put your lives on the line. There is nowhere to run. Communication is slow, inaccurate, and often mistaken. Don't become dispirited. Provide the information

that is needed. Take in what is happening now, but also look five hours, ten hours, a day, a week ahead, and act accordingly. It doesn't matter how much it costs. No one can do this but TEPCO. When Japan is at risk of failure, withdrawal is out of the question. Mr. Chairman and Mr. President, prepare yourselves. Employees who are over sixty should go to the site. I, too, will work with this commitment. Withdrawal is out of the question. If you withdraw, TEPCO will inevitably fail.

At around 6 a.m. that day, while I was still at TEPCO's headquarters, we received reports that a large crashing noise had come from the vicinity of the suppression chamber in the Unit 2 reactor. It appears that extreme pressure caused a hole to form somewhere in the suppression chamber. If the entire reactor containment vessel had been destroyed, the worst would have followed.

In every respect, TEPCO had fallen behind. Their headquarters, in particular, was not functioning properly. Watching a video conference call, I came to understand that important supplies such as batteries had yet to reach the site several days after the accident occurred. With the formation of the Integrated Response Office, it became easier for TEPCO to obtain cooperation from the Self-Defense Forces and the police, and matters improved greatly.

Ever since the accident, we had been under attack from radiation. But starting on March 16, the day after the establishment of the Integrated Response Office, the Japan Self-Defense Forces began sending in helicopters to drop water on the site. Because airborne radiation levels were high, the airlifting of water was postponed for a day, but on the seventeenth a last-ditch effort was made, and the area was flooded with water. With this forward momentum, there was an improvement in the morale of the Self-Defense Forces, firefighters, police, and others, a new determination to put their lives on the line to save Japan. And the United States, the military in particular, showed a new eagerness to provide full support if the Japan Self-Defense Forces took the lead.

Furthermore, either because of venting or a hole that had formed—it remains unclear which—the pressure in the Unit 2 reactor dropped and the injection of water became possible. As a result, we were able to cool the reactor, and as the temperature fell, it became more stable.

By the Grace of the Gods

If the reactor containment vessel had exploded, bursting like a balloon, the worst-case scenario would have been unavoidable. But the structure as a whole remained intact, and a single, concentrated release of lethal quantities of radioactive materials did not occur.

While the efforts of those on-site played a significant part in our dodging of total destruction, ultimately I think we benefited from a combination of good fortune and chance. One such bit of good fortune was the presence of water in the spent fuel pool at the Unit 4 reactor. Because construction work on the site was behind schedule, Unit 4 was full of water, and it is thought that some sort of impact caused this water to spill into the spent fuel pool. If the water in the pool had come to a boil and evaporated, the worst-case scenario could not have been averted. This was surely divine intervention.

As a result, the worst-case scenario never materialized, and I did not have to order the evacuation of 50 million people. But ever since, the worst-case scenario has remained a permanent presence in the back of my mind.

Support from the United States

I want to outline here the role that the United States played as Japan faced its worst crisis since World War II. At fifteen minutes after midnight on March 12, I received my first telephone call from President Obama. After expressing his condolences, he reassured me with his statement that "we want to provide you with every possible assistance." Immediately after the disaster, the United States initiated "Operation Tomodachi [Friend]." On March 13, the USS *Ronald Reagan* nuclear-powered aircraft carrier arrived off the coast of Fukushima and started providing rescue assistance to victims of the earthquake and the tsunami.

On the morning of the twelfth, in the midst of this chaos, the press reported that the Japanese government had turned down an offer by the United States to provide us with a cooling agent for the nuclear reactors at Fukushima. Although it was later confirmed that this had been a false report, the chief cabinet secretary was kept busy straightening out this and other negative reporting based on false information. Reports also circulated that the United States had requested that their nuclear experts be located in the prime minister's compound and included in strategy meetings, but the chief cabinet secretary had turned them down. In the interest of national sovereignty it would have been unheard of for foreign specialists to sit in on strategy meetings attended by the prime minister, but a room had been provided in the prime minister's compound for meetings of specialists from both of our governments.

From the time of the accident at the Fukushima nuclear power plant, the US government showed a keen sensitivity to impending danger. Having experienced the accident at Three Mile Island in 1979 and the 9/11 terrorist attacks in 2001, the United States was particularly well prepared to manage a crisis of this nature and scale. A large number of US citizens live in Japan, and in keeping with the US-Japan Security Treaty, the largest US overseas military bases are located here. Consistent with this relationship and immediately after the accident at Fukushima's Daiichi Nuclear Power Plant, the US government rushed in nuclear experts, particularly members of the Nuclear Regulatory Commission. They also brought in experts in Japanese diplomacy who initiated their own analysis of the situation.

In the first days after the nuclear accident, Japan was unable to provide the United States with concrete findings, and the Americans suspected that the Japanese government was withholding information. Early on, the United States Air Force located in Japan deployed a Global Hawk reconnaissance drone to independently measure temperatures and radiation levels at the Fukushima site. Apparently, the dearth of similar information coming from Japan increased their suspicions. In fact, the Japanese government was not intentionally hiding anything. The reality was that for a time after the accident occurred, we did not have an accurate understanding of conditions on-site.

The first nuclear experts from the United States arrived in Japan on March 13. On the following day, they were greeted at the prime minister's compound by deputy chief cabinet secretary Tetsuro Fukuyama. They were also joined by representatives of the Nuclear Safety Commission (NSC) and NISA. This meeting extended over the following two days, and they were given an explanation that I assume was nearly identical to what I and others in the prime minister's office had been given as well. Thereafter, the United States and Japan continued to communicate intermittently. In the course of these discussions, the Americans found discrepancies between the information they had gathered and the picture being painted by their Japanese counterparts. I believe this may have deepened their suspicions that the Japanese were not being open with them. Furthermore, the Americans feared, early on, that the Japanese government was leaving the handling of the accident entirely in the hands of TEPCO. It had been my understanding, from the moment I heard the Fukushima plant was without electricity, that this nuclear accident was a crisis of national proportions. I knew that the reactors would melt down if we were unable to cool them and that if the nuclear fuel were to escape, this would result in extremely high radiation levels that would require the evacuation of an extensive area.

With the establishment of a liaison office in the prime minister's compound, the creation of a joint command center, with repeated telephone communication between the chief cabinet secretary Yukio Edano and deputy chief cabinet secretary Fukuyama and US assistant secretary of state Kurt Campbell and US ambassador John Roos, and as a result of other efforts to share information, I believe the US government's initial distrust was gradually dispelled. Beginning on March 22, all related personnel from the United States and Japan met regularly to assure effective communication. From the United States, these meetings were attended by representatives of the US Embassy in Tokyo, the NRC, the Department of Energy, and so on. On the Japanese side, in addition to Deputy Chief Cabinet Secretary Fukuyama and Special Adviser Hosono from my offices, meetings were attended by representatives of the Ministry of Economy, Trade, and Industry (METI), the Nuclear and Industrial Safety Agency, the Ministry of Foreign Affairs, the Ministry of Defense, and so on. Representatives of TEPCO participated as well.

These meetings led to the implementation of US knowledge and technical assistance, such as the flooding of the reactors, the use of robots specifically designed for disasters, the delivery of barges, and the like. Furthermore, in late March, US experts in radiation medicine came to Japan and, working as part of a Japan-US joint task force, created a report. Through the accumulation of such efforts, collaboration between the United States and Japan improved.

When a country's citizens are in danger overseas, it is common to counsel them to leave, and shortly after the nuclear accident occurred, US government officials discussed the evacuation of most of the Americans residing in Japan, members of the armed forces included. There would have been significant political implications if the military were evacuated from Japan, and apparently such matters were deliberated by US government officials insofar as they would affect US-Japanese relations. Ultimately, based on radiation estimates, the US government encouraged only the evacuation of US citizens within an eighty-kilometer [fifty-mile] radius of the Fukushima nuclear power plant.

Following the earthquake disaster, I received sympathetic calls and offers of cooperation from the heads of many other countries in addition to the United States. Among them, France's president Nicolas Sarkozy offered to send nuclear experts and said that he would like, even if for a short time, to visit Japan as well. Given the constraints on my time, I declined his offer of a visit at that time. But France's rather forceful requests continued, and given that they were scheduled to host the next G8 summit in May, we approved a visit by President Sarkozy on March 31. It came to pass that we received technical assistance from France as well.

A Glimpse at Japan's Destruction

Since stepping down from the role of prime minister, I have been repeatedly asked, "Did you think of yourself as unfortunate to have had such a major accident occur when you were the prime minister?" I did not think in terms of good or bad luck. I neither lamented it nor did I see it as an opportunity to make my mark. I thought of it as my fate, and as such I could not run from it. That is what I told myself.

After the accident occurred, Chernobyl was constantly on my mind, so when I set out to write this book I took a look at the memoirs of Mikhail Gorbachev, a fellow politician who had also come face to face with hell. His account of Chernobyl closely resembled my own experience, so I would like to share several short excerpts from his book.

> During these days, we felt intuitively, since we still did not have complete information, that this was a very dramatic situation with potentially serious consequences.
>
> Based on what I know, I would never suspect any of these individuals of having an irresponsible attitude towards the fate of the people. If something was not done in a timely manner, it was mainly because of a lack of information. Neither the politicians, nor even the scientists and specialists, were prepared to fully grasp what had happened.
>
> The closed nature and secrecy of the nuclear power industry, which was burdened by bureaucracy and monopolism in science, had an extremely bad effect. I spoke of this at a meeting of the Politburo on 3 July 1986: "For thirty years you scientists, specialists and ministers have been telling us that everything was safe. And you think that we will look on you as gods. But now we have ended up with a fiasco. The ministers and scientific centres have been working outside of any controls. Throughout the entire system there has reigned a spirit of servility, fawning, clannishness and persecution of independent thinkers, window dressing, and personal clan ties between leaders.
>
> In our country there were a few who tried to treat Chernobyl as a subject for political speculation.[3]

Gorbachev's account reveals a close resemblance to the situation in Japan. Five years after the accident occurred, the Soviet Union collapsed. Although Gorbachev and I had both looked into the abyss of a major nuclear accident, we reached completely different conclusions about the future of nuclear power.

In contrast to Gorbachev's judgment that nuclear power is necessary, I resolved to abandon it.

An End to the Use of Nuclear Power

After experiencing the March 11 nuclear accident at Fukushima Daiichi, many people have shared their views regarding nuclear power. I recall the philosopher Takeshi Umehara's penetrating description of the Fukushima nuclear accident as a "disaster caused by civilization" at the first meeting of the Reconstruction Design Council in 2011.

The question of our relationship with nuclear power is not simply a discourse on technology or economics. It is a critique of the way we live, a critique of our culture. It can be said that accidents at nuclear power plants are disasters brought on by mistakes in judgment that our culture, our very civilization, is making. If this is true, that is all the more reason to say that ultimately the question of whether or not to phase out nuclear power is not as much rooted in technology as it is in the will of the people. One could say that this is a philosophical matter. I too, as one who experienced the March 11 nuclear accident, think it is unrealistic for humans to make use of nuclear reactions, and I have come to think of nuclear energy as a threat to our very existence.

There is a well-known story in Greek mythology about Prometheus's fire. My father raised me on that story, telling it to me a number of times beginning when I was in grade school. Prometheus had taught the human race about fire. This angered Zeus, who said, "If you give fire to mankind, it will be the cause of much trouble," and Zeus tied Prometheus to a rock to suffer for all eternity, pecked at daily by an eagle. My father had a white-collar job in a technical area, but apparently he had loved literature as a young man. In the course of hearing this story many times, I came to think that it was the role of government to control Prometheus's fire.

I should add that one reason I became a politician was the existence of nuclear weapons. In 1957, scientists and intellectuals from around the world had gathered for the first Pugwash Conference. This meeting was largely inspired by Albert Einstein, Bertrand Russell, and Hideki Yukawa, who had expressed their regrets with regard to the development of the atom bomb and had joined together to urge the elimination of atomic weapons. I learned of this conference when I was a student and was made aware once again that science and technology are not able to bring harmony to mankind.

While we continue to make scientific and technological progress, the abilities of the individual have not evolved a great deal. And as long as that gap exists, there will be occasions when we lose control of science and technology. The development of nuclear weapons is one such paradox, a self-contradiction that could be likened to a mouse building a mousetrap. Whether humans will ever demonstrate the wisdom to adopt or reject science and technology has concerned me since I was young. This was where my involvement in politics began. Even though the Tokyo Institute of Technology was a science school, my interest in politics and my involvement in the student movement, my participation in citizens' movements after graduating, and my decision to become a politician all came from a desire to do something about the contradictions inherent to science and technology.

Humans and all other living things here on Earth exist in the good graces of the sun. With the exception of geothermal energy, all the energy we have used comes from our sun. And there are those who say that the sun's energy finds its origins in nuclear fusion. But the sun is some 150 million kilometers [93 million miles] from the Earth. This distance weakens the radiation generated by the sun's nuclear reactions to the point that it has almost no effect on humans. Looking at it from another angle, we could say that the life forms that are born and endure life here on Earth, humans included, are limited to those that are capable of coexisting with the weakened radiation that comes from our distant sun.

Contrary to our sun, which exists in nature, can we coexist with the nuclear energy–generating devices we have created over the past several decades? Can we coexist with nuclear weapons and nuclear power? I think that if mankind fails, the cause will be nuclear. Developments in science and technology are endangering our very existence; therein lies the greatest contradiction.

Personally, at all costs, I want to see an end to the use of nuclear power. And as a politician who experienced the Fukushima nuclear accident as the prime minister, I feel it is my duty.

1

Memories from the Abyss

I would like now to look back in greater detail at the week immediately following the Great East Japan earthquake.

March 11 (Friday)

The Swinging Chandelier

At 2:46 p.m. on March 11, 2011, when the Great East Japan earthquake occurred, I was attending a meeting of the Audit Committee of the House of Councillors, the upper house of the National Diet of Japan.

The opposition Liberal Democratic Party held a majority in the House of Councillors at the time, meaning that we had a "twisted" Parliament [in which the upper and lower houses were separately controlled]. Even the schedule for deliberations was determined at the insistence of the opposition, and the prime minister was to spend long hours fielding questions at meetings of the Standing Committee on Budget and the Audit Committee. Regarding the budget, in keeping with the constitution, the House of Councillors is in a superior position. In recent years the Standing Committee on Budget has enjoyed particular prominence.

Traditionally, the Audit Committee is to have a question-and-answer session regarding the settlement of the accounts and the administration of the previous year's budget. But the questioning on this day was not with regard to the settlement of the accounts per se. Rather, there was a concentrated focus on a political contribution I had received, and I was attacked with great intensity. The problem was a donation from a foreigner[1] [in Japan, it is illegal to accept donations for political purposes from foreign nationals or foreign organizations] among the contributions I had reported.

At 2:46 p.m., in the midst of what was, for me, harsh questioning, the earthquake struck, and a violent shaking continued for quite some time. The chandelier hanging from the ceiling of the committee chamber swung violently. Fearing that it would fall, I remained seated, clinging to both arms of my chair and looking upward.

After a long period, when the shaking finally ceased, the committee chair Yosuke Tsuruho declared a recess, and I departed immediately for the prime minister's compound. On arriving, I went directly to the Crisis Management Center in the basement. The chief cabinet secretary was already there, and other related personnel arrived soon after in quick succession.

When an earthquake with a magnitude of six or greater occurs, a response team is automatically established in the office of the prime minister. This emergency team is under the auspices of the deputy chief cabinet secretary for crisis management and is made up of bureau chiefs from each of the ministries. Because Tetsuro Itoh, deputy chief cabinet secretary for crisis management, was in the prime minister's compound at the time of the earthquake, he had immediately convened the emergency team. Deputy Chief Itoh was formerly the chief commissioner of the Metropolitan Police and had also assumed the office of deputy chief cabinet secretary for crisis management during the Yasuo Fukuda administration in 2008. During that same year he had experienced the Iwate-Miyagi earthquake [that struck the Tohoku area on the morning of June 14, 2008].

Emergency Disaster Response Headquarters

The response team meeting began at 3:14 p.m., shortly after my arrival. Deputy Chief Itoh opened with "Our current concern is the establishment of an Emergency Disaster Response Headquarters," and I immediately agreed.[2] A cabinet meeting is necessary for the establishment of an Emergency Disaster Response Headquarters given that this headquarters has a great deal of authority. The director-general (the prime minister) may issue orders if the need arises not only to the central government's ministries but to the local governments as well. The headquarters comprises all the cabinet ministers and vice ministers and any heads of designated administrative agencies the prime minister wishes to appoint. The prime minister is the director-general; and the ministers of disaster management, defense, and internal affairs and communications are the deputy directors.

We could not fathom the overall damage caused by the earthquake but sensed that this was the largest earthquake to have struck Japan in the postwar era and began to prepare the relief effort. First we determined policy for the saving of lives. It is said that in the case of a major earthquake, the first seventy-two hours is key. Remembering that the Self-Defense Forces had been late to arrive at the site of the Great Hanshin earthquake in 1995, I immediately asked Minister of Defense Kitazawa to dispatch the Self-Defense Forces. We received word from the Ministry of Defense that they could commit twenty thousand personnel right away, so

I ordered the deployment of twenty thousand. Worried this might not be enough, I asked Kitazawa to consider the possibility of dispatching more.

Station Blackout

Immediately after the Great East Japan earthquake struck, TEPCO shut down all the reactors at Fukushima's Daiichi and Daini nuclear power plants. At Fukushima Daiichi, reactor units 1, 2, and 3 were all being operated at the time, while reactor units 4 through 6 were shut down for routine periodic inspections. But when a huge tsunami struck the Sanriku coast, one after another the reactors at Fukushima Daiichi lost their power.[3]

Enacted in 1999, the Act on Special Measures Concerning Nuclear Emergency Preparedness [hereafter Nuclear Emergency Preparedness Act] establishes how one should deal with a nuclear accident or a nuclear disaster. In Japan, nuclear reactors were first commercially used in 1966—beginning with the Tokai Nuclear Power Plant in Ibaraki Prefecture—but there were no regulations for the handling of nuclear disasters until 1999. The Nuclear Emergency Preparedness Act was enacted when, in September 1999, an accident occurred at the Japan Nuclear Fuel Conversion Co. (JCO) fuel preparation plant in Tokaimura. This accident did not involve a nuclear reactor. Rather, it was caused by a company that handled spent nuclear fuel, and two workers died from acute radiation exposure. Prior to the accident it had been assumed that an accident would not occur at a nuclear power facility, hence the absence of legislation regarding the role of the government in the event one did occur. The Nuclear Emergency Preparedness Act supposes that in the event of a severe accident, the operator (the electric company) is responsible for the reactors and other on-site facilities—for the containment of nuclear accidents—while the national and local governments are responsible for the evacuation of nearby residents and other off-site matters.

In keeping with the Nuclear Emergency Preparedness Act, when a nuclear emergency has been declared, a Nuclear Emergency Response Headquarters is established with the prime minister as its director-general and METI's Nuclear and Industrial Safety Agency as its secretariat. The collection of information and decision making takes place at an off-site center for emergency response measures located near the site. When an accident occurs, all related personnel gather at this off-site center, create a local strategy headquarters, determine the approach they will take, and take action after gaining the approval of the prime minister.

Declaration of a Nuclear Emergency

I attended a meeting of the Emergency Disaster Response Headquarters together with the entire cabinet. When it ended, at 4:22 p.m., I returned to my office. At this time I was already scheduled to hold my first press conference after the earthquake and to meet with the heads of the ruling and opposition parties. Prior to these commitments I had meetings with the Democratic Party's secretary-general Katsuya Okada and its acting leader Yoshito Sengoku.

At 4:54 p.m., at the first press conference after the earthquake, I spoke of the earthquake, offered my condolences, reported the establishment of the Emergency Disaster Response Headquarters, and said that we would be doing everything in our power to keep the damage to a minimum. I said that a portion of a nuclear power plant had automatically shut down but that nothing was known with regard to radioactive materials.

Although this was a press conference, I did not take questions, so it was over in about four minutes, and I returned immediately to my office on the fifth floor of the prime minister's compound. A discussion with special advisers Hosono and Terada and a representative of NISA that began around 5 p.m. was joined by METI's minister Kaieda at 5:42 p.m. Minister Kaieda reported to me regarding conditions, as stipulated in article 15 of the Nuclear Emergency Preparedness Act, and submitted a written statement requisite to the declaration of a nuclear emergency.

It goes without saying that the declaration of a nuclear emergency was required by law, but I also wanted to learn as much as I could about the status of the accident. In the middle of the explanation, I excused myself for five minutes for a scheduled meeting with the heads of the ruling and opposition parties. After returning and listening to a further explanation of the situation, I declared a nuclear emergency at 7:03 p.m. Then I established a Nuclear Emergency Response Headquarters and commenced its first meeting.

Later I was criticized for allowing too much time to pass between the METI minister's written statement and my declaration of an emergency, but in fact an Emergency Disaster Response Headquarters had already been established and the Crisis Management Center was in a state of preparedness. With regard to the nuclear accident as well, a response group had already been established within the prime minister's compound. Prior to the formal creation of the Nuclear Emergency Response Headquarters, information was being gathered, the parameters of our authority were being confirmed, and other practical business was being attended to. In no particular respect were we tardy in our response to the nuclear accident.

In the Crisis Management Center in the basement of the prime minister's compound, the Nuclear Emergency Response

Headquarters and the Emergency Disaster Response Headquarters were set up adjacent to one another.

The position of director-general of the Nuclear Emergency Response Headquarters is filled by the prime minister with the minister of the Ministry of Economy, Trade, and Industry as the deputy director-general. Furthermore, all other members—the number is not stipulated—are appointed by the prime minister from among the remaining cabinet members. The deputy chief cabinet secretary for crisis management, the vice ministers, and the heads of designated administrative agencies are also appointed by the prime minister. The administrative staff is appointed by the prime minister from among the cabinet secretariat, the staff of designated administrative agencies, and the heads or members of the staff of designated local administrative agencies. Basically, the members are almost entirely the same as the members of the Emergency Disaster Response Headquarters, with NISA being the only organization that is only represented in the Nuclear Emergency Response Headquarters.

In fact, meetings of the Emergency Disaster Response Headquarters and the Nuclear Emergency Response Headquarters were often held concurrently. For example, the fifth meeting of the Tohoku Region Pacific Offshore Earthquake Disaster Response Headquarters and the third meeting of the Nuclear Emergency Response Headquarters might be held at the same time. Just the same, a nuclear accident and an earthquake and tsunami are quite different in nature. While for earthquakes and tsunamis the greatest crisis comes at the time of their occurrence, with nuclear accidents the greatest concern is the degree to which the accident will grow. With earthquakes and tsunamis one is addressing something that has already happened, but with nuclear accidents one must anticipate what will happen and act accordingly. So the two response headquarters had to work from two different perspectives and with two different approaches.

This was true of the evacuation of local residents as well. There was no choice but to relocate those whose homes had collapsed in the earthquake or were washed away by the tsunami. But in the case of a nuclear accident, a person's house might remain unscathed, and yet we still had to move them out. And while the Emergency Disaster Response Headquarters had to administer to an extensive geographical area, the Nuclear Emergency Response Headquarters had only to consider the immediate vicinity of the Fukushima Daiichi Nuclear Power Plant.

At any rate, in addition to an unprecedented earthquake and tsunami, we came face to face with the first-ever severe accident involving several nuclear reactors. This was two national crises at once. We had experienced the Great Hanshin earthquake and others too, but this was the first severe accident involving multiple reactors the world had ever seen. No one had ever experienced this before.

Authority and Responsibility

According to article 25 of the Nuclear Emergency Preparedness Act, when an accident occurs, the operator must take the necessary emergency precautions to offset the occurrence or expansion of a nuclear accident. The Fukushima Daiichi Nuclear Power Plant is owned by TEPCO, which is a private company. In other words, the plant is private property and the employees are all private citizens. So what authority does the state have with regard to this private property and these private citizens? We had to be prepared to make a decision in this regard.

A report prepared by the National Diet of Japan Fukushima Nuclear Accident Independent Investigation Commission [NAIIC] has made issue of this matter of intervention on the part of the prime minister's office and the prime minister, and I would like to share my thoughts in this regard.

First, I would like to make a point with regard to the prime minister's legal authority. According to article 20 of the Nuclear Emergency Preparedness Act, when emergency measures are deemed necessary, the prime minister, as director-general of the Emergency Disaster Response Headquarters, may direct or instruct the plant's operator (TEPCO) as required. In this case, the word "instruct" carries some weight, and insofar as TEPCO is a licensed organization, it would be unheard of for them not to submit to the prime minister's orders. Therefore, it is inaccurate to suggest that an individual who would not normally have authority is coming along, out of nowhere, and intervening. According to law, the director-general of the Nuclear Emergency Response Headquarters is able to give instructions. Although I might be criticized for the content of the instructions I gave, it is not right to call my giving of instructions an inappropriate intervention.

Second, I would like to address the responsibilities of the prime minister in the face of a national emergency. While certainly, according to the law, the prime minister may give instructions to TEPCO "when it is deemed necessary," great discretion is required when determining whether or not something is necessary. Generally speaking, I believe that authority should be wielded as little as possible.

In that respect, it was unprecedented that during the four days from the time of the accident until the establishment of the Government-TEPCO Integrated Response Office, the prime minister's office was directly involved and played a central role in the effort to contain the accident. But while it was certainly highly unusual, when an emergency on the scale of a national crisis occurs,

I believe the prime minister should make use of every conceivable form of authority and do everything in his or her power to head off a crisis. This was a severe accident that neither TEPCO nor the Nuclear Industrial Safety Agency had anticipated. It was my understanding that conditions were such that I, as the prime minister, should wield my authority. Below I will outline in detail my handling of the accident so that you can be the judge.[4]

The Nuclear Safety Commission

The Nuclear Emergency Preparedness Act also states that the director-general of the Nuclear Emergency Response Headquarters "may request of the nuclear power plant's operators and other related entities the provision of materials and information, the expression of opinions, and other cooperation." It was for this reason that I asked for a representative of TEPCO who was capable of explaining matters to be stationed in the prime minister's office.

Continuing in this vein regarding the director-general's authority as defined by the Nuclear Emergency Preparedness Act, when it is determined that the quick and unerring execution of an emergency response is necessary, the director-general may request of the Nuclear Safety Commission [NSC] the necessary advice regarding technical matters toward the execution of emergency response measures. Based on this, the NSC stationed its chairman, Haruki Madarame, in the prime minister's offices nearly full time, and he advised us.

The NSC is a deliberative council that broke off from the Japan Atomic Energy Commission in 1978. The Japan Atomic Energy Commission was established in 1955 in keeping with the Atomic Energy Basic Law. Its mission is to plan, deliberate, and decide on basic policies and strategies for the promotion of the research, development, and utilization of nuclear energy; to coordinate the administrative activities of related organizations; to compile the budgets for these organizations; and to advise the related ministers regarding the regulation of nuclear fuel, nuclear reactors, and so on. The Japan Atomic Energy Commission is also a gathering of nuclear specialists, but the Nuclear Emergency Preparedness Act, which was created as a guideline for the response to a nuclear accident, says nothing of the role of this commission.

The NSC was established in 1974 when the nuclear battleship *Mutsu* leaked radioactive material. Later, in response to an accident involving the handling of uranium in Tokaimura, Ibaraki, in 1999, the commission's function and organization were further developed and strengthened. The commission was made independent of METI and the Ministry of Education, Culture, Sports, Science, and Technology [MEXT], and from this more neutral position they developed a fundamental approach to national safety regulations and have taken on the role of supervising government organizations and plant operators. With the ability to make recommendations to government organizations that have direct access to the prime minister, the NSC has a great deal of authority. Five commission members, the chair included, are appointed by the prime minister and approved by the Diet. Beneath these five members are 250 specialists in a variety of committees: a sixty-member committee of reactor safety experts, a forty-member committee of nuclear-fuel safety experts, a forty-member committee for the study of emergency response measures, and so on. The commission's secretariat has a staff of one hundred.

Returning to the evening of March 11, after establishing a Nuclear Disaster Response Headquarters in the Crisis Management Center, in order to understand the status of the accident, I asked for representatives of NISA, the NSC and TEPCO who were able to explain the situation to come to the prime minister's office. According to the Nuclear Emergency Preparedness Act, the prime minister is the director-general of the Nuclear Disaster Response Headquarters, but the actual administration of the response to the nuclear accident is handled by NISA, which takes on the role of the headquarters' secretariat, with their director-general as the secretary-general.

With the exception of people with a connection to nuclear power, prior to this accident probably very few people were aware of the existence of NISA, an organization born out of a reorganization of the central government in 2001. In addition to the agency's headquarters, which is located in Kasumigaseki, there are twenty-one nuclear-safety inspector offices and nine industrial safety and inspection departments, with a total of eight hundred personnel spread throughout Japan. There is a nuclear-safety inspectors' office in the Okuma Township, near the Fukushima plant, and this was where the off-site nuclear disaster-strategy headquarters was to be located.

Learning from the experience of the Tokaimura JCO Criticality Accident, the Nuclear Emergency Preparedness Act made an effort to locate the response team as close to the accident site as possible. With this in mind, the off-site headquarters near the Fukushima plant was to serve as an operational center where information was gathered and decisions were made, but the earthquake and radiation had incapacitated it.

While the Nuclear Emergency Preparedness Act anticipates a state of emergency at the nuclear facility, it supposes a peaceful state elsewhere. But this time all of eastern Japan was in a state of emergency, an emergency that was being caused, in part, by the accident that was unfolding at a nuclear facility in the region.

METI's deputy minister Motohisa Ikeda, who was supposed to be the director of the local off-site disaster-strategy headquarters, was stuck in a traffic jam caused by the earthquake and was very late arriving. He was not the only person who was late. Local government employees were also supposed to convene at the off-site center but insofar as the area had been struck by an earthquake and tsunami they were in no condition to do so. Electric outages, damaged roads, and cut lines of communication also made it impossible to contact those who should come to the off-site headquarters. And when contact was possible, the poor condition of the roads often impaired the person's arrival. Employees from six surrounding government offices were supposed to support the effort, but only employees of the Okuma Township [within which a portion of the plant is located] were able to come. To make matters worse, the off-site center itself had no electricity and no lines of communication. As a result, with regard to the initial response to the accident, the off-site center was not able to function as planned, and ultimately, on March 15, the local disaster-strategy headquarters was moved to within the Fukushima prefectural government office.

The Nuclear Emergency Preparedness Act specifies that the local disaster-strategy headquarters, situated in the off-site center, decides on the area to be evacuated and the prime minister, as the center's director-general, then approves of this and other proposals that have come from them, from the bottom up. That is the prime minister's role. However, conditions were such that there was no bottom, so there was no choice but to work from the top down. Actually, there was no "down" to go to, so the top (the prime minister's office) had no choice but to do the work.

The Nature of the Nuclear and Industrial Safety Agency

The Nuclear and Industrial Safety Agency handled the safety inspection of nuclear and other energy facilities but was not prepared to respond to an accident. The Nuclear Emergency Preparedness Act mainly gives NISA responsibility for the gathering of information (a continuation of their peacetime duties) and the provision of technical advice to the prime minister in his capacity as the director-general of the Nuclear Emergency Response Headquarters.

As an elected official I, too, was and still am responsible for the fact that while Japan has more than fifty nuclear reactors, it does not have a single organization that specializes in the containment of a nuclear accident. And the fire and police departments are not prepared either. The Self-Defense Forces have the Central Nuclear Biological Chemical Weapon Defense Unit, which trains to handle an attack making use of nuclear and other weapons. They were dispatched in response to this accident, but they did not have any direct knowledge regarding the containment of a nuclear accident. The reason there is no organization for the containment of a nuclear accident is because an accident was not supposed to occur. And I suppose the creation of such an organization by the government could have been seen as an admission that an accident might occur, which might then have impeded the further construction of nuclear power plants.

I thought the staff of NISA would naturally be made up of nuclear power experts. Based on my experience as minister of health, labor, and welfare and as minister of finance, those bureaucracies were composed of specialists in the areas they were responsible for. In the Ministry of Health, Labor, and Welfare there were experts in pensions, medicine, nursing, and so on. In the Ministry of Finance there were experts in taxation, finance, and the like. For this reason I thought NISA would be made up of specialists in nuclear safety.

When NISA's director-general Nobuaki Terasaka came along and described the situation to me, I was left with a strange impression. It does not take long to discern whether a person who is explaining something really knows what they are talking about.

Listening to Director-General Terasaka, I could not comprehend what he was trying to tell me, so I asked him, "Are you a specialist in nuclear power?" To this he replied, innocently, "I'm a graduate of the University of Tokyo's Economics Department."

NISA is a special organization related to the Agency for Natural Resources and Energy, which is an external agency of METI, and while the field staff are probably experts, the management positions are filled by career bureaucrats from METI. As METI bureaucrats, they are versed in economics but amateurs in the field of nuclear power. I believe the top management of NISA should be specialists in nuclear power. If they are not, they should at least be accompanied by a specialist when they visit the prime minister to explain a nuclear accident. Particularly in the case of a serious accident such as this one, I wanted to know what might happen to the reactors and the likelihood of a meltdown. I also wanted for there to be a full consideration of what could be done to prevent a meltdown from occurring and whether such actions were being taken. The answers were meaningless in the absence of an expert.

I was not interested in talking with someone with a science background just because I happen to have one. The fact that many politicians are educated in the humanities is all the more reason it is a problem if you are not able to explain nuclear power to a novice in a way they can understand. Otherwise one finds oneself in a situation where neither the politician asking the questions nor the top of NISA has a detailed understanding of what is going on.

On the next NISA visit, the vice director-general who came to my office in place of Director-General Terasaka had a background in science, although he was not an expert in nuclear power. Three days after the initial accident, in need of an expert in nuclear power, we brought in Masaya Yasui, the director of the Agency for

Natural Resources and Energy at METI. As our adviser from NISA, he explained matters to us.

Power

In the face of a severe accident, problems kept occurring that TEPCO could not resolve on their own. When we asked TEPCO's liaison Ichiro Takeguro to keep us informed of the situation but also if there was something we could do, he said, "We really need power-supply trucks."

Ordinarily, in preparation for a blackout, a backup power source for the emergency cooling mechanisms should have been placed in an elevated location. But it just so happens that at the Fukushima Daiichi Nuclear Power Plant the emergency diesel generators were located in the basement, so when the tsunami struck, they were flooded and rendered useless.

When this occurred, TEPCO suggested that if power-supply trucks [mobile generating units] were brought quickly, the emergency cooling apparatus could be operated while the original electrical source was being repaired. Power-supply trucks located at several other TEPCO facilities were apparently on the way. A request had also been made to Tohoku Electric, and Deputy Chief Cabinet Secretary Tetsuro Fukuyama had contacted the Ministry of Defense in an effort to get as many power-supply trucks as possible to Fukushima.

Under more peaceful conditions, TEPCO probably would have contacted another of their plants to secure and move the trucks. But as with the deputy minister of economy, trade, and industry, who got stuck in a traffic jam on his way to the off-site center, the condition of the roads was terrible. The heart of Tokyo was jammed, and in the disaster area there was a good chance the roads had caved in or been wiped out by landslides. The highways were closed to use by private vehicles, making transport by regular means difficult.

To move the trucks smoothly, it was necessary for the police and Self-Defense Forces to lead them in convoys. But at a time when there was already a state of confusion, even if TEPCO had been able to contact the police, the police would probably not have been able to act on their behalf. This is where the Nuclear Emergency Response Headquarters in the office of the prime minister could be of help, making full use of organizations like the police and the Self-Defense Forces, and making the movement of power-supply trucks a national emergency of the highest priority.

A power source was necessary to cool the reactors. Everyone knew that if cooling stopped, the reactors would eventually melt down. At this point, getting power-supply trucks to the site as soon as possible was critical, and because NISA and others were not functioning as they normally should have, the offices of the prime minister, myself included, had no choice but to handle this matter directly.

In the beginning, we made use of a portion of the Crisis Management Center in the basement to cope with the nuclear accident. There was a small room, large enough for about ten people, in the basement's "mezzanine" (a room half under and half above ground level). Because its location made it easy to receive word regarding the earthquake, the tsunami, and the nuclear accident, we made use of it. But there were only two telephones, and for security reasons cell phones could not be used, so I stayed in my office on the fifth floor where I could receive calls. The other political-affairs staff were in the mezzanine at first, but before long they were gathering on the fifth floor as well, and it became the strategy headquarters' command center for all intents and purposes.

The staff brought a whiteboard into the office and wrote down the current locations of the various power-supply trucks that were hurriedly making their way to the Fukushima Daiichi Nuclear Power Plant. They recorded the exact time a given truck passed a certain exit on the highway, and in no time the whiteboard was black.

Around that time someone had the idea of airlifting a power-supply truck with a helicopter, so I asked one of my private secretaries who was originally from the Defense Ministry to look into it. When we tried the idea out on the US military, they said it would not work because the trucks were too heavy.

After 9 p.m. we received word that the first power-supply truck had arrived on-site. When we received the news, a cheer rose up from the area around my office. It felt like when a goal is scored at a soccer match at the World Cup or the Olympics. Everyone present thought this meant we could keep the accident from getting worse, that we had evaded a crisis. But our happiness was short-lived.

We would learn later that the power-supply truck's plug did not fit. It could not be attached to the power source, the cable was not long enough, and they were not able to use the power-supply board. The generator we had worked so hard to arrange was of no use. We were astonished to learn that TEPCO—a collection of electricity specialists—had not thought to confirm whether the power-supply truck was compatible.

Venting and Evacuation

Beginning around 9 p.m., in the basement "mezzanine," I discussed the evacuation of residents with METI's minister Kaieda, Special Adviser Hosono, and personnel from TEPCO, the NSC, and

NISA. It was decided that we would evacuate everyone within three kilometers [1.9 miles] of Fukushima Daiichi and ask those between three and ten kilometers [1.9 and 6.2 miles] to remain indoors.

At 9:23 p.m., the Nuclear Emergency Response Headquarters ordered the evacuation of the area within a three-kilometer [1.9 mile] radius of the nuclear power plant. Later we would learn that Fukushima Prefecture had already independently ordered an evacuation of residents within two kilometers [1.2 miles] of the plant at 8:50 p.m. The Fukushima prefectural office and the Nuclear Emergency Response Headquarters had not been in contact with one another. The order to evacuate a three-kilometer area was announced to the general public in a press conference held by Chief Cabinet Secretary Edano that began at 9:52 p.m.

At 10:44 p.m. the Crisis Management Center in the prime minister's office received a forecast from NISA regarding the Unit 2 reactor. At 10:50 p.m. the reactor core would be exposed, at 11:50 p.m. the fuel assembly cladding would be compromised, and at 12:50 a.m. the fuel would melt. Conditions were extremely grave.

March 12 (Saturday)

Open the Vents!

Midnight came and went, and it was now March 12, a Saturday. For several days, beginning on the eleventh, I had no sense of what day of the week it was. I also did not have a sense of when yesterday ended and today began. Time passed, unpunctuated.

I spoke with President Obama at 12:15 a.m. I think it was after that that I told Executive Secretary Kenji Okamoto and Special Adviser Terada that "there's a chance I will go to Fukushima in the morning, so please make preparations."

NISA felt that the Unit 2 reactor was in trouble, but that at this point the Unit 1 reactor was in even greater danger. At 12:06 a.m. the plant manager Masao Yoshida had given orders to prepare for the venting of the Unit 1 reactor. TEPCO requested our consent, and we began discussing this matter shortly after 1 a.m. I believe this meeting was attended by TEPCO's liaison Takeguro, Chairman Madarame, Minister Kaieda, Chief Cabinet Minister Edano, Deputy Chief Cabinet Minister Fukuyama, NISA's vice director-general Eiji Hiraoka, and others. We did not hesitate where venting was concerned. If anything, we wanted it done as soon as possible. It was my understanding that by venting we could avoid an explosion. We could buy time during which, with the use of power-supply trucks, the cooling mechanism could be restored and the worst could be avoided.

When I asked how long it would take to begin venting, TEPCO's liaison Takeguro told me, "Preparations will take two hours," so it was my understanding that the venting would be possible by about 3 a.m. At 9:23 p.m. on the previous day, I had already issued an order to evacuate the area within three kilometers of the plant, but the pressure in the reactor had risen since then. Since the power-supply truck was not compatible with the pump, the problem of cooling remained unresolved. Conditions were growing worse.

Having assumed that the vent could be opened by 3:00 a.m., Chief Cabinet Minister Edano and Minister Kaieda had each prepared press conferences. In fact, at 3:06, Kaieda and Komori had begun a press conference at the Ministry of Economy, Trade, and Industry, and at 3:12 Edano had initiated a press conference at the prime minister's offices. At Edano's press conference he announced that I would visit the site, departing at 6:10 a.m. At this point I had already decided that I would visit the Fukushima Daiichi Plant and also view, from above, the areas that had suffered damage from the tsunami. I had a schedule made accordingly. I should add that even at a time of emergency such as this one, when a prime minister goes anywhere, an elaborate schedule is prepared in advance and he is expected to proceed accordingly. Improvising is generally frowned upon.

I have always been a hands-on person. I believe leaders should confirm matters with their own two eyes before making a decision. Being pressed to make decisions that would affect the people's lives and the country's fate, I felt that a firsthand knowledge of the source of these problems was of the greatest importance.

I did not know what was going on at the plant. Nor did I know if our thoughts and inclinations were reaching the people on-site. Regardless of what I asked the TEPCO employees who came to the prime minister's office compound, it always took time for them to get back to me. And when I asked a follow-up question, they were unable to answer me on the spot and the process started all over again. It was like "telephone" or some other "pass-the-message" game. Information was passed from the plant to TEPCO headquarters, from headquarters to NISA, from NISA to the office of the prime minister or to a TEPCO employee stationed there. It would have been fine if the messages were accurate, but somewhere along the way some important piece of information would get lost, and there was always the possibility of a distortion, however unintentional.

It was for this reason that I had decided to visit the site, even if for a short time, and get a direct report from the person in charge. With regard to the paying of a visit, it is true that there were those among my staff who felt I should be more circumspect. In particular, I recall Chief Cabinet Secretary Edano's reluctance to endorse a visit. He was not against it because of administrative problems that might arise from my absence. Rather, I recall his saying that

I should not go because of potential political fallout later. I think Edano was worried that my reputation would suffer, but I did not care about that. I just felt the need to go to the site and grasp the situation directly, taking it all in with my own eyes and ears. It was for that reason that I had decided to go.

Another risk was the possibility that, by visiting the site, I would be exposed to radiation. And one could not entirely eliminate the chance of an explosion. I did not have any precise scientific basis for it, but I did not believe I would suffer from acute radiation syndrome or any other condition that would impair my work as prime minister. In the event of a disaster, the timing of the prime minister's visit to the site is always a matter of debate. If one waits for several days, people complain, saying, "What are you doing here now?" And if you go immediately, you are told, "The site is in a state of confusion, and your visit is making it even more so." Generally speaking, there are two approaches to a crisis. The commander either leads or sits tight with great composure and leaves matters to his staff.

As Chief Cabinet Secretary Edano had feared, this visit to the site of the accident was criticized at the Diet, but I am confident I made the right decision. Because I visited the site at that point in time, I was able to meet with the person in charge, the plant manager Yoshida. I was also able to ascertain the chasm that existed between the site and TEPCO headquarters and was, therefore, compelled to enter TEPCO headquarters at the break of dawn on the fifteenth. And although I disembarked only at Fukushima Daiichi, I was able to see the damage caused by the tsunami from the helicopter. There had been little information from the areas struck by the tsunami. The local town and city government buildings had themselves been hit, and most of their communication lines had been severed. I had seen footage on television, but I felt that I needed to see it directly to understand the scale of the disaster.

At around 5 a.m. I went down to the Crisis Management Center in the basement. When I arrived, Deputy Chief Cabinet Secretary Fukuyama informed me that the venting had yet to begin. I was surprised because I had assumed it was already well under way. I would learn later that it had to be done manually, and high radiation levels were impeding progress.

I asked Chairman Madarame, "What happens if we're unable to vent? Isn't there a risk that the reactor containment vessel will explode?" Hearing this exchange, Chief Cabinet Secretary Edano and Deputy Chief Cabinet Secretary Fukuyama suggested extending the evacuation area from a three-kilometer to a ten-kilometer radius, and I agreed with them. The records show that it was 5:44 a.m.

The War Zone

At 6:14 a.m. I departed from the roof of the prime minister's offices in the Super Puma, a Self-Defense Forces helicopter. I was joined by Dr. Madarame, chairman of the NSC, and I asked him all manner of questions. I carried a notebook and took notes, and I clearly recall asking, "Is there any danger of a hydrogen explosion?" to which the chairman answered with conviction, "Even if hydrogen is released within the reactor containment vessel, the vessel is full of nitrogen. In the absence of oxygen, an explosion is out of the question."

Prior to this, TEPCO's employees and NISA's staff had all said, "I don't know," a response that I and other elected officials found exasperating. So when Chairman Madarame stated confidently that "an explosion is out of the question," I was put at ease. This would turn out to be a big mistake, however.

We arrived at the Fukushima Daiichi Nuclear Power Plant at 7:12 a.m. It had taken us more than an hour. The helicopter landed on something resembling a playing field, and we boarded a bus that had been prepared on our behalf. TEPCO's vice president Sakae Mutoh and Deputy Minister Ikeda of METI, who was also the government's representative on-site in his capacity as director of the Local Off-Site Disaster Strategy Headquarters, boarded the bus as well. Deputy Minister Ikeda, who had been caught in a traffic jam as I described above, had finally managed to arrive in the middle of the night. The fact that this off-site headquarters did not properly function was something the law had failed to predict.

Vice President Mutoh sat beside me on the bus, so I asked him why they were unable to open the vents. When he failed to respond, I raised my voice in anger. I definitely was agitated on that occasion. I believed that this nuclear accident had placed the very existence of our country in danger, and our ability to evade a crisis was dependent on the vents. While I was living with that sense of danger, the vice president—who I assumed was in a position of responsibility—was only offering a half-baked response. If venting was not possible, I wanted to know why that was the case. In the absence of a clear explanation, I raised my voice.

After some time passed, we arrived at a seismically isolated building. The entrance to this structure was two-staged and when we passed through the first set of doors, someone shouted angrily, "Come in quickly!"

We had arrived in a war zone. The hallway was full of workers, a number of whom were lying on the floor. Some were wrapped in blankets, others were bare from the waist up. Nearly everyone had a blank stare. It was what I imagined a field hospital would be like. This quake-resistant building had become a rest area for workers who had completed their shifts. One could infer that they had worked in a severe environment through the night.

Many of the workers had collapsed on the floor, leaving just enough room for one person to pass, so we walked single file. We had been told there was a conference room on the second floor, so we headed toward the stairs, but before we knew it, we found ourselves standing at the back of a long line. At first I thought the line was not moving forward merely because the hall was congested and there was no room to pass. We stood there like that for a while until we learned that it was a line for workers to measure their radiation exposure. I was reminded of the need to balance a response to the accident with a full consideration of the safety of those performing the work.

Yelling out, "What's going on? We don't have time for this. We're here to see the plant manager," I left the line and pushed my way through the workers, moving forward until I had found the stairs to the second floor. In the conference room there was a large table and monitor, and on the table was a map of the Fukushima Daiichi Nuclear Power Plant.

Plant manager Yoshida entered immediately after. He was a completely different type of person from the TEPCO employees I had encountered at the prime minister's office. He explained the situation in his own words, saying, "Because motor-operated venting will take another four hours, we are now considering whether or not to attempt this manually, and I hope to make a decision in the next hour."

I had initially been told that the venting would begin at 3 a.m. Four hours had already passed since this scheduled time, and now he was telling me that we would have to wait another four hours. Wasn't it TEPCO who had spoken of the need to vent in the first place? When I said, "We can't wait that long. Can't you do it faster?"

plant manager Yoshida said, "I will create a suicide squad to do the work." This plant manager was different from the vice president, who had only mumbled a vague response.

While I had risked political criticism and an exposure to radiation, the biggest benefit derived from my decision to visit the site at this point in time was that I was able to get a sense of the person who was running the site, namely plant manager Yoshida. Since the time of the earthquake, I had received very little reliable information. I did not know if my orders were really reaching those who were working on-site. I did not know what was reaching them and what was not. In making decisions, it is important to know that orders are being effectively conveyed to the concerned party. Because this was unclear, I had wanted to confirm this directly myself.

NSC chairman Madarame was not making decisions based on a direct observation of the site. He had been to the Fukushima Daiichi Nuclear Power Plant, but that had been several years ago. I also did not know the extent to which NISA grasped the situation. Even TEPCO, who should have had the most firsthand information, was conveying this to me through a chain of intermediaries, so even when I asked, it was unclear who was making the decisions and who was responsible for them. Everything had been conducted with anonymity. When I met plant manager Yoshida, I felt that I had finally found someone who would talk straight with me.

Records show that we departed the plant at 8:05 a.m., so we were there for a little under one hour. During that time, at 7:45, they had lost the ability to control the pressure in the nuclear reactors at the Fukushima Daini Nuclear Power Plant as well, and a state of emergency was declared. The area within three kilometers of Fukushima Daini was designated an evacuation area, and residents between three and ten kilometers from the plant were ordered to stay indoors. This decision was made while we were visiting Fukushima Daiichi. At Fukushima Daini, two of three electricity transmission systems had been knocked out, and the tsunami had caused the reactor cooling mechanisms to malfunction. Without reaching the point of exploding, all the reactors at Fukushima Daini achieved a cold shutdown on the fifteenth, but until then we could not rest at ease.

Departing Fukushima, I observed from the helicopter the disaster areas in Miyagi and Iwate prefectures. This trip would prove to be of value in my later handling of matters, not only for what I learned at the nuclear power plant but from what I was able to confirm, albeit from the air, of the damage that had been caused by the tsunami.

Of course, I had seen the damage caused by the earthquake and tsunami on television, but that was edited footage. Looking with my own two eyes and in all directions, I was able to appreciate just how dreadful the damage was. Along the shore, conditions were such that I could not differentiate between the ocean and the land. Initially I had wanted to land, but this would have required people on the ground to make preparations to receive me. Even though I would not have desired such, when a prime minister visits, that is what happens. Furthermore, I had to return to the prime minister's compound in Tokyo later that morning, so it had been decided that we would go as far north as possible within the time allowed.

Recognizing that most of the damage incurred by this earthquake had been caused by the tsunami, I determined the need for maximum relief, so when I returned to my office, after discussing the matter with Minister of Defense Kitazawa, I ordered the deployment of fifty thousand members of the Self-Defense Forces. On the previous day I had asked about the potential for an increase in personnel and had been told that up to fifty thousand troops could be made available. That is why I ordered the commitment of this number of troops.

Knowing that I was asking a lot of him, I prevailed upon Minister Kitazawa to increase the number even more. The minister took note and conferred on my behalf with key officers of the Self-Defense Forces. As a result, on the following day, the thirteenth, I received word that they had committed a maximum of one hundred thousand troops to the relief effort. As the total number of members of the Self-Defense Forces is 240,000, this was a little less than half. A hundred thousand troops was the maximum number of personnel to be committed in the event of a major earthquake in the Tokyo metropolitan area. Because the Self-Defense Forces had been preparing for such an event for some time, they were able to respond quickly.

I arrived at the prime minister's compound at 10:47 a.m. Entering my own office on the fifth floor, I was greeted by Deputy Chief Cabinet Secretary Fukuyama. I said to him something along the lines of "Plant manager Yoshida is all right. We can trust him. I can talk with that man." For me, the harvest had been great.

Learning of an Explosion, on Television

Plant manager Yoshida said that he would open the vents even if it required the creation of a suicide squad, and apparently the work was death-defying. At 2:30 that afternoon they succeeded in reducing the pressure in the reactor containment vessel. I was relieved when I received reports that while some radioactive material was being released, we were gradually extricating ourselves from this crisis situation.

But according to a subsequent announcement by TEPCO and an investigation by the National Diet of Japan Fukushima Nuclear

Accident Independent Investigation Commission, at around 7 p.m. on the eleventh, nuclear fuel in the Unit 1 reactor core had begun to fall to the bottom of the pressure vessel, and it is thought that a meltdown was under way. So we do not know for sure whether the reduction in pressure that was reported at 2:30 p.m. on the twelfth resulted from venting or from a meltdown.

Beginning at 3 p.m., I met with the leaders of the majority and minority parties. We agreed to pool our energies toward reconstruction. This meeting ended a little bit after 4 p.m.

Immediately after, I received a report from Deputy Chief Cabinet Secretary for Crisis Management Itoh: "The sound of an explosion was heard at the Fukushima Daiichi Plant, and it is giving off smoke." But Mr. Itoh did not seem to know any more than that. I decided to have the matter explained to me in detail in my office. I was joined there by Chairman Madarame, Deputy Chief Cabinet Secretary Fukuyama, and the vice minister for policy coordination Kenichi Shimomura.

After a short time, we received word that, rather than white smoke, something black was sprinkling down. I called in TEPCO's liaison Ichiro Takeguro and asked, "What's going on?" He said, "I have not heard. I will ask headquarters," and placed a phone call. He then told me, "They're saying they don't know anything about it."

When I asked Chairman Madarame, "What do you think the smoke is coming from?" he answered ambiguously, "There are lots of volatile things on-site, and it would seem that one of them is on fire." At that point Special Adviser Terada came in with a worried look on his face and said, "Turn on the television right away!" On the screen we saw the Unit 1 reactor building exploding. I was at a loss for words. I recall Vice Minister Shimomura asking Chairman Madarame, "What was that just now? Wasn't that an explosion?" The chairman had both hands covering his face.

It wasn't just white smoke. No matter how you looked at it, it was an explosion. Deputy Chief Cabinet Secretary Fukuyama asked Chairman Madarame, "Was that explosion on the scale of Chernobyl?"

I would learn later that the explosion had occurred at 3:36 p.m. It was first reported by the local news media and then broadcast nationally by its affiliate Nippon TV at 4:50 p.m. When I saw it on television, it was Nippon TV's coverage that I saw. This is to say that more than an hour after the explosion I had not received any word from either TEPCO or NISA. Nippon TV had taken time to confirm matters after receiving footage from their affiliate in Fukushima, and this had further delayed its broadcast.

I ordered my executive secretary to "Get me some information quickly!" The time for Chief Cabinet Secretary Edano's press conference was approaching. Everyone in the country, in the world for that matter, already knew of the explosion in the Unit 1 reactor, but we had no information with which to provide an explanation to the people. Yet a delay in the press conference would probably make people all the more anxious.

Chief Cabinet Secretary Edano was criticized for his artifice in saying "an explosion-like event" at this press conference, but in the absence of an official report from TEPCO or NISA that made use of the word "explosion," the Nuclear Disaster Response Headquarters could not conclude that an "explosion" had occurred.

Why the Expansion of Evacuation
Zones Was Incremental

At 5:44 a.m., we had already established a ten-kilometer evacuation zone for Fukushima Daiichi. With regard to Fukushima Daini, at 7:45 a.m., during my visit to Fukushima Daiichi, orders were given to evacuate an area within three kilometers and to remain indoors between three and ten kilometers, but at 5:35 p.m. the evacuation area for Fukushima Daini was extended to ten kilometers. This measure was taken because, like Fukushima Daiichi, there was the possibility an explosion would occur at Fukushima Daini.

This expansion of the evacuation zone was announced by Chief Cabinet Secretary Edano at his press conference. Sometime later we received word that the explosion at the Unit 1 reactor was not an explosion of the reactor containment vessel but of the structure surrounding the reactor, and that it was a hydrogen explosion, not a nuclear explosion. When I asked Chairman Madarame, "Didn't you tell me that a hydrogen explosion would not occur?" he responded with something like, "When I said a hydrogen explosion would not occur, I was referring to an explosion within the containment vessel, not the reactor building."

In his book *Nuclear Crisis: A Testimony from the Prime Minister's Office*, Deputy Chief Cabinet Secretary Fukuyama wrote that Chairman Madarame admitted to having been consumed by thoughts of the condition within the reactor containment vessel and had not considered that hydrogen might escape into the reactor building and cause an explosion there.

At 6:25 p.m. we further expanded the evacuation zone around Fukushima Daiichi, ordering an evacuation within a radius of twenty kilometers [12.4 miles]. At this point in time the cause of the explosion in the Unit 1 reactor had yet to be confirmed, and units 2 and 3 were also in a dangerous state.

This gradual expansion of the evacuation zone was met with criticism at the time, but a threefold increase in the radius means a ninefold increase in the area. Taking Fukushima Daiichi as an example, 5,862 people were living within a three-kilometer radius of the plant. Move the radius out to ten kilometers, and there were more than fifty thousand residents. At twenty kilometers there were more than 170,000.

If we evacuated a ten-kilometer zone from the start, and everyone in the area moved at once, there was a good chance that the closer a person lived to the plant, the longer it would have taken for them to flee. So we had no choice but to start by evacuating those in the greatest danger—those living within three kilometers—and when that area had been vacated, to expand the area to ten kilometers, and when that evacuation was complete, to move to twenty kilometers. However, because we chose this method, people who had been evacuated once were forced to evacuate again, causing greater confusion and resulting in greater criticism. This was one of many experiences we need to reflect on and learn from.

Around this time I began to wonder, if things continued in this vein, just how far we would have to extend the evacuation zone. Watching footage of Fukushima Daiichi, I was concerned by the proximity of reactor units 1 through 4. Because each of the buildings is quite large, one does not get an impression of crowding, but I felt that, given their size, they were too close to one another. If Unit 1 were to melt down, causing a release of highly radioactive material, not only would we be unable to approach Unit 1, but Unit 2 as well, and eventually Unit 3, and so on in a chain of negative events.

At Fukushima's Daiichi Nuclear Power Plant alone there are six reactors, and in addition to spent fuel pools at each of the units there is a shared pool, making for a total of seven. Given the quantity of spent nuclear fuel contained therein, there was a possibility that the evacuation zone would have to be extended as far as Tokyo. If that were to happen, how would we evacuate?

The Truth about Seawater

After the explosion in the Unit 1 reactor building, Chairman Madarame suggested, with regard to Unit 1, "Let's cool the reactor by submerging it in seawater."

Because it was suggested later at the Diet that I had halted the injection of seawater, I would like to address this matter thoroughly here. To come right to the point, neither I nor anyone in the office of the prime minister gave an order to stop the injection of seawater at any time. If anything, we gave orders to hurry up.

Beginning sometime before 6 p.m., I was conferring with Minister Kaieda, Chairman Madarame, management from NISA, and TEPCO's liaison Ichiro Takeguro. At that point in time, the specialists agreed that if we ran out of fresh water, we would have to use seawater for the purpose of cooling. I did not have any objection to this, but I did ask several questions. Because a hydrogen explosion had occurred even though I had been told that one would not, there were points of concern I wanted to clear up. For example, was there a possibility that with the introduction of seawater, the salt would corrode the reactor?

I was also concerned about recriticality. Recriticality is when the melted nuclear fuel exceeds a certain size, causing a chain reaction to occur once again. When I asked about the possibility of recriticality, in keeping with the quantity of nuclear fuel that had melted down, Chairman Madarame said, "It isn't completely out of the question." I interpreted Chairman Madarame's statement at this time to mean that there was a risk of recriticality.

Finally, I said, "If it will take two hours before the seawater can be injected, during that time please look into the potential influence of salt. And if there is a risk of recriticality, consider the addition of boric acid, which absorbs neutrons and apparently makes it more difficult for recriticality to occur." Asking them to please consider these and other matters, I left the meeting. I never said a word about delaying or stopping the introduction of seawater. Because I was told that they could not begin until two hours later, all I did was ask Chairman Madarame and the representative from NISA to think things over in the meantime. Furthermore, I did not suggest that if seawater was injected, it would cause recriticality. Rather, I asked them to consider the problem of damage caused by salt when injecting seawater and, independently, to consider the possibility of recriticality and the measures to be taken. I asked them to think about these two distinct problems. This was distorted when it was reported.

It came to be known later that the introduction of seawater began at 7:04 p.m., but that action had not been reported to me. I would learn after the fact that Mr. Takeguro, the TEPCO liaison, had called plant manager Yoshida in keeping with my request to confirm the situation, and was informed that the infusion of seawater had already begun. Mr. Takeguro said, "Because we have not received the approval of the prime minister, please wait," and then called TEPCO headquarters, after which the headquarters ordered Yoshida to stop. Yoshida pretended to follow these orders but continued to inject seawater.

I was still unaware of these machinations at TEPCO at 7:40 p.m. when Special Adviser Hosono brought me radiation-monitoring data from Fukushima's Daiichi. Radiation levels were highest at the moment of the explosion and had dropped thereafter. I interpreted this to mean that rather than a nuclear explosion, a hydrogen explosion had occurred. Things did not appear to be as bad as they might have been.

After I received this report, a meeting was held to determine whether or not to introduce seawater. I was told, "If boric acid is added, recriticality is not a problem." Not knowing that seawater was already being injected, I ordered its introduction at 7:55 p.m. At this point seawater had already been injected for more than fifty minutes.

Consequent inspections would reveal that the meltdown [of the Unit 1 reactor] had already occurred at 8 p.m. on the previous day, March 11.

A Message to the People

At 8:30 p.m., one and a half days after the earthquake had occurred, in order to confront the worst national crisis Japan had faced since the war, I decided to address the Japanese people. I spoke first of our complete dedication to the rescue effort in the wake of the tsunami, and then, in light of recent developments at Fukushima Daiichi, I requested further evacuation. Finally, I appealed to the people to overcome this national crisis.

I have included a record of those points below.

At six o'clock this morning, I visited the site of the disaster in a Self-Defense Forces helicopter. I first went to the Fukushima Daiichi Nuclear Power Plant and was briefed in full by personnel there. In addition, I thoroughly inspected Sendai, Ishinomaki, and other such areas from the helicopter. It became clear to me that because this earthquake was accompanied by a major tsunami, it brought with it immense damage and heavy losses.

With regard to our lifesaving efforts, yesterday, today, and tomorrow we must put all of our energy into this rescue work. I have asked the Self-Defense Forces to commit fifty thousand troops rather than the initial twenty thousand, and I just met with Mr. Kitazawa, the minister of defense, and asked him to consider a further commitment, making use of personnel from around the country. To save as many lives as possible we must commit ourselves completely to see ourselves through today, tomorrow, and the day after.

Many people have already been evacuated to shelters. We are making every effort to provide the disaster-stricken area with food, water, and, because this is a very cold time of year, blankets and heaters, in addition to toilets and other facilities. In this way we are doing everything we can to help all who are victims of this disaster to overcome this situation, and we ask for your perseverance.

In addition, many are worried about the Fukushima Daiichi and Daini nuclear power plants. Because the tsunami resulting from this earthquake far surpassed the maximum size formerly predicted, we have had problems with backup generators that were supposed to function in the event of a power failure. For this reason we have taken steps that place the safety of the citizens first.

In particular, with regard to Fukushima Daiichi's Unit 1 reactor, there are new developments that the chief cabinet secretary will explain in detail hereafter. In keeping with this situation, while we had already requested the evacuation of a ten-kilometer area, I would like to ask now that everyone within twenty kilometers of the Fukushima Daiichi Nuclear Power Plant evacuate the area. We will be making every effort through this and other substantive actions to keep any and all citizens out of harm's way. With this in mind, I sincerely hope that you will take note of information provided by the government and the press, and that you act with composure.

(text omitted)

Citizens of Japan, the strength of each and every one of you and the total commitment of the government-related organizations you support must help us overcome this earthquake disaster, this truly unprecedented national crisis. I hope that, in the various situations you find yourselves in, you will persevere and take actions you can look back on and say that it was out of our hard work that a new Japan was born. I ask this of all of you, and I promise that I will put my own life on the line, devoting body and soul to this effort. Please, I ask this of you.

A meeting of the Emergency Disaster Response Headquarters and the Nuclear Emergency Response Headquarters was held beginning at 9:34 p.m. The rescue of victims of the earthquake disaster was also an important problem, and there was a pressing need for the arrangement of evacuation centers. Some of the local government buildings had collapsed or were washed away, mayors and local government employees were themselves victims of the disaster, and we had absolutely no idea what was going on in some areas. We did not even fully understand the extent of this unprecedented disaster.

The most important political decision to be made by a prime minister in response to a disaster is the commitment of Self-Defense Forces personnel, and with regard to this matter, I did not hesitate. As described above, immediately after the earthquake, I had asked Defense Minister Kitazawa to dispatch the largest possible number of personnel. Twenty thousand were dispatched immediately, and ultimately one hundred thousand of the total force of 240,000 were mobilized. Defense Minister Kitazawa also traveled to the disaster area by helicopter on March 14, and, after observing that the power of the tsunami had surpassed anything he had imagined, he felt that the decision to commit one hundred thousand troops had been correct. He wrote of this in his book *Why Japan Needs the Self-Defense Forces*.

Getting a Second Opinion

By nature, the work of a prime minister is not administrative. It could be said that a prime minister's most important jobs are "thinking" and "decision making." During this period, most of my thoughts were about the extent to which the nuclear accident might grow and how it might be stopped.

After the meeting of the Emergency Disaster Response Head-quarters and the Nuclear Disaster Response Headquarters, I was visited in my offices by Yasushi Hibino, a classmate from Tokyo Institute of Technology. I had been trying to reach him since the previous day, and when I finally did I had imposed on him to visit me.

Ever since the nuclear accident occurred, in addition to ideas from NISA and other organizations that were by nature set up to address such matters, I had wanted a second opinion from outside experts. Fortunately, my alma mater, the Tokyo Institute of Technology, has a nuclear power research laboratory and many experts in the field. I could not remember offhand anyone among my closer classmates who was an expert in nuclear power, but I figured that if I extended the circle out to friends of friends, there would be some experts among them. I was looking to create a team of brains who could provide me with a second opinion.

With this in mind, I contacted Mr. Hibino, who had come to a gathering of Tokyo Institute of Technology classmates several days before. Mr. Hibino was an electrical engineer. After working for many years at an NTT [Nippon Telegraph and Telephone Corporation] research laboratory, he had joined academia and become vice president of the graduate school at the Japan Advanced Institute of Science and Technology. Even back when we were students he was someone you could count on. He was quite composed and in possession, from the outset, of a wide range of scientific and technical knowledge. Because he was to retire from the university at the end of March, I had asked him if he might become a special adviser to the cabinet with regard to science and technology. Subsequently, Professor Masanori Aritomi, director of the Research Laboratory for Nuclear Reactors at the Tokyo Institute of Technology, and Professor Masaki Saito also agreed to participate as advisers. I also interviewed Kenichi Ohmae at my office and asked him to become an adviser. He responded that he did not want to take a position that involved the protection of privileged information but would cooperate privately.

Most information from government organizations was the result of deliberations by the related parties, and for this reason it took time to prepare and tended to be ambiguous. In contrast, the recommendations I received from the experts who acted as my advisers were prompt, personal, and exceedingly helpful.

March 13 (Sunday)

Sleeping at the Office

While I held the office of prime minister I lived with my wife and eighty-nine-year-old mother in a building on the grounds of the prime minister's compound. This building had originally served as the work quarters of the prime minister but had since been moved and renovated. The distance from the front door of the office building to the entrance to the residence was 110 paces, and the round-trip walks between the two were among the few opportunities I had to walk anywhere.

Prime ministers are rarely permitted to walk. While "permitted" is a strange way of putting it, the security detail encouraged movement by car. It is uncommon for a prime minister to go out to meet someone. Rather, when meetings do occur, the prime minister greets guests at the official compound. The only place the prime minister commonly goes out to is the Diet building, and though it is very close at hand, even then a car is always provided.

Because the offices and residence are quite close, if an emergency were to occur I could have run from one to the other in a matter of minutes. But until the nuclear accident settled down, I did not return home. Instead, I lay on a couch in a reception room behind the office I used for official duties. It is my understanding that the political staff and bureaucrats working for Chief Cabinet Secretary Edano also spent those days without rest or sleep.

On the night of the twelfth I slept at the office again. It was more like a nap. Around eight o'clock in the morning, Special Adviser Hosono brought me a memo. During the middle of the night and into the early hours of the morning, conditions at reactor Unit 3 had progressively worsened. At 5 a.m. the emergency core-cooling system that had somehow continued to flood the reactor core had ceased to function. TEPCO reported that reactor Unit 3 now also met the conditions for a nuclear emergency as specified in article 15 of the Nuclear Emergency Preparedness Act.

Reports on the eleventh had been with regard to units 1 and 2. At that time the emergency cooling system in Unit 3 was still functioning. But we were no longer able to flood the core, the water had evaporated, and it was overheating. The memo predicted "a meltdown shortly after 8 a.m." Then, shortly before 9:30 a.m., Special Adviser Hosono came to report, "We have succeeded with the venting of reactor Unit 3," and told me that a reduction in pressure had been confirmed.

The Necessary Weapons

A little after 11 a.m. Toshiba's president Norio Sasaki arrived. Having been advised by Mr. Hibino the previous evening that reactor core manufacturers would be the most knowledgeable, and hoping to ask for their assistance with the containment of the accident, I had contacted him and asked him to come. President Sasaki told me that he was an expert in nuclear power, so I promptly asked him to explain the situation.

Of the six reactors at Fukushima Daiichi, Toshiba had manufactured four: units 2, 3, 5, and 6. Units 2 and 6 were made in collaboration with US General Electric. Unit 1 was made by General Electric alone, and Unit 4 was built by Hitachi.

When I asked President Sasaki his diagnosis of the situation, he readily told me, "There is a possibility of a hydrogen explosion in reactor units 2 and 3." When I asked whether a hole might be cut in the roof to allow the hydrogen to escape, he told me, "A spark might set off an explosion, so the use of a water jet would be the best way to cut it."

Unlike my conversations with TEPCO headquarters and with NISA personnel, President Sasaki answered briskly. I asked him to "take the proper measures," and wouldn't you know it, he told me, "We already gathered from around the country those items we thought would be needed—high- and low-tension cables, high voltage transformers, circuit breakers, and the like. Some of this equipment has already arrived at J-Village,[5] but because we're not allowed to go beyond that point, we're unable to reach the plant."

Certainly no one was to enter the evacuated area, and it was right for the police to be stopping all vehicles. But if TEPCO had informed NISA, and NISA had informed the Nuclear Disaster Response Headquarters, this problem could have been solved immediately. Ideally, they should have been provided with a police escort and allowed to pass through. Calling on the police, the Self-Defense Forces, and all other related organizations in the country, we had created a Nuclear Disaster Response Headquarters in the cabinet. But it was not functioning.

I called in my executive secretary immediately and directed the Toshiba vehicles to be given access. It was not my job to work on-site. My job was to make final decisions. But I was not receiving any reports or proposals. It was difficult to discern what was happening. It was when I had occasion for some reason or other to have direct contact with the outside world that I was first able to understand the situation.

An article in *Asahi Shimbun* [a national newspaper] on September 5, 2012, established that TEPCO had not functioned well. According to the article, "The situation was made worse by the fact that TEPCO's hands were tied with regard to gathering on-site enough powerful fire trucks, fire-truck drivers and operators, batteries, fuel, and other materials. There was also a temporary shortage of the cash necessary for the procurement of materials. If they had been able to somehow gather the equipment and personnel, there was a chance they could have prevented the meltdown of the cores in reactor units 2 and 3. We at *Asahi* came to understand this through an inspection of TEPCO's video conferences."

When I read this article I remembered plant manager Yoshida's statement "Just give us the *weapons*." I cannot accurately recall at what point it was, but Mr. Yoshida had said this to my aide, Mr. Hosono, when they spoke on the telephone about how dire conditions were on-site. According to *Asahi*, "having suffered a calamity, the very water, kerosene, gasoline, batteries, and fire trucks that were needed to respond had difficulty reaching the site of TEPCO's Fukushima Daiichi Nuclear Power Plant. To make matters worse, the people who were able to operate the fire trucks and other heavy machinery worked for subcontractors and could not be given orders in the manner that regular employees could." The weapons plant manager Yoshida had needed there on the front lines had not arrived.

TEPCO's Top Management Absent

At 1 p.m., at the introduction of [my college classmate and adviser] Mr. Hibino, Professor Koichi Shimada of the Nuclear Reactor

Core Research Laboratory at the Tokyo Institute of Technology came to visit. After explaining developments since March 11, I asked for the comprehensive help of my alma mater. Professor Shimada consented and promised to "gather nuclear power experts," making a trip to the university for that purpose. The creation of a second-opinion team had become a possibility. Because I knew the Tokyo Institute of Technology's president Kenichi Iga quite well, I also called him up and asked him to make preparations to provide us with support.

After Professor Shimada departed, at 1:45 p.m. I met with TEPCO's president Shimizu for the first time. On the day of the accident he had been in Kansai [the area in and around Osaka], and Chairman Tsunehisa Katsumata was in China on business. This meant that TEPCO's top two executives were absent at the time of the disaster.

After meeting with President Shimizu, I spent the remainder of the afternoon meeting individually with the leaders of Japan's political parties and taking telephone calls from the leaders of various countries. At 2:45 p.m. I met with Mr. Sadakazu Tanigaki, president of the Liberal Democratic Party. At 3:30 I spoke on the telephone with Korea's president Lee Myung-bak. At 3:55 I spoke with Australia's prime minister Julia Gillard. At 4:30 I met with Mizuho Fukushima, head of the Social Democratic Party, and at 5:00 I met with Shizuka Kamei, representative of the People's New Party.

The Japan Meteorological Agency announced that the earthquake on the eleventh had a magnitude of 9.0. It had been assessed at 8.8 at the time, so this was a revised estimate. The energy exerted by the quake was approximately forty-five times that of the Great Kanto earthquake [in 1923] and 1,450 times that of the Great Hanshin earthquake [in 1995]. Among the earthquakes that had occurred worldwide since the year 1900, it was the fourth largest.

It was thought that the deaths would number in the tens of thousands. The Self-Defense Forces and police and fire departments were giving their all to relief, search, and rescue work, but conditions were severe. There were reports of difficulties getting relief supplies to the evacuation shelters, and, although all branches of the government were doing everything they could, there were areas in which we fell short.

Masaru Sato's Blog

On March 13, 2011, the writer and critic Masaru Sato wrote the following about the position I was in, in his blog (also to be found in "March 11 Crisis," *Magazine World*):

> Even from mass media's suppressed reports, the people can divine that the Fukushima Daiichi Nuclear Power Plant is in critical condition. The prime minister must take whatever action is necessary without fear of its extralegal nature. Under these circumstances, we, the people of Japan, must be acutely aware that it is our duty to risk our lives in order to rescue the country from a national crisis. Since the war, our national order has been built on modernism. Central to that order is a belief in the supremacy of life and the rights of the individual. Nothing is more important than the life of the individual, and the nation cannot ask its citizens to give up their lives. But if one thinks in terms of international standards, it is clear that, regardless of the country, there are occupations that demand unlimited liability of the individual. Unlimited liability is when the performance of one's duties is more important than one's own life.
>
> In Japan, based on the nature of their work, members of the Self-Defense Forces and the Coast Guard, police officers, firefighters, and foreign-service officers bear the burden of unlimited liability. Under normal circumstances, we would not imagine unlimited liability for those who are working for or related to TEPCO. But in

light of the state of emergency at the Fukushima Daiichi Nuclear Power Plant, this is a time when people with expertise are expected to risk their own lives and make every effort to save us from disaster. The news media has not reported on this in detail, but Japanese nuclear power experts are on-site, risking their lives to extricate us from this crisis. In an effort to circumvent this crisis, Prime Minister Kan must not hesitate to give extralegal orders demanding unlimited liability. As Japan's democratically selected leader, Prime Minister Kan should follow his professional conscience and do everything necessary for the survival of Japan and its people.

Rolling Blackouts

That afternoon another major problem presented itself. As the earthquake had occurred on a Friday and was immediately followed by a weekend, many businesses had been closed. But we could anticipate that Tokyo—which had suffered little damage—would return to business as usual when Monday arrived. Because the earthquake and tsunami had incapacitated the Fukushima Nuclear Power Plant and some thermal power stations were unable to generate electricity, the region serviced by TEPCO was expected to suffer from a significant power shortage. When demand exceeded supply, there would be no avoiding major blackouts. TEPCO was telling us that to avoid this, there was no alternative to rotational shutdowns (rolling blackouts).

Chief Cabinet Secretary Edano and Deputy Chief Cabinet Secretary Fukuyama took a firm stance with TEPCO in this regard, so the company did not entirely get their way, but many citizens and businesses would be inconvenienced. To handle the rolling blackouts, I appointed Renho, minister of state for government revitalization, as the minister for electricity conservation promotion. Furthermore, I asked Diet member Kiyomi Tsujimoto to become an aide to the prime minister taking responsibility for all volunteer work.

To explain these and other matters, I held a press conference beginning at 7:49 p.m. [and opened with the following statement]:

This is the night of the third day after the earthquake. I want to express my heartfelt sympathies to all who have suffered as a result of this disaster. Beginning with the areas struck and extending to all Japanese citizens, I want to express my gratitude and my sincere respect for your composure during these particularly trying times.

Throughout the day today, we continued to commit all our resources to the rescue effort. Thus far, with the help of the Self-Defense Forces, police, firefighters, Coast Guard, and other organizations from overseas, we have been able to save some twelve thousand people.

Our current rescue operation involves fifty thousand members of the Self-Defense Forces working on land, at sea, and in the air. And we are preparing to increase this number to one hundred thousand personnel. More than 2,500 police officers, from around the country, are also in the disaster area. As for firefighters and emergency personnel, more than 1,100 crews are on location. We have also dispatched more than two hundred disaster-relief medical teams. Because the overland routes are limited, we are considering the use of air and sea routes for the transport of food, water, blankets, and the like, and committing a lot of resources to this effort. Furthermore, we have designated this a severe disaster and are considering additional, legal action.

Meanwhile, with regard to the Fukushima nuclear power plant, which is a source of anxiety for everyone, conditions remain critical. Chief Cabinet Secretary Edano will provide a detailed report in this regard shortly. Fellow citizens, there is something I want for you all to understand, and something I want to ask of you. The Fukushima nuclear power plants and many other power-generation plants have suffered damage, making it exceedingly difficult to supply electricity to the areas serviced by TEPCO and Tohoku Electric.

The government has instructed other electric companies to supply these two companies with electricity and the like, and we are asking the utmost of them. In addition, we are asking businesses and families to conserve electricity.

As there is no chance of recovery in the near future, and without greater effort, we can anticipate that we will suffer from a shortage of electricity and possibly be reduced to blackouts on a large scale, in the entire region. As sudden and major blackouts would deal a significant blow to people's daily lives and to any business enterprise, we want to do whatever possible to keep them from occurring. Toward this end, I have reached an agreement with TEPCO for the implementation of rolling blackouts, beginning tomorrow, in the area they serve. The minister of economy, trade, and industry will explain the details hereafter. I have come to this decision with great reluctance, knowing how inconvenienced the public will be. Not only will electricity be shut off, but gas, water, and other lifelines may be affected, and there may conceivably be an adverse effect on the use of medical and healthcare equipment as well.

In order to carefully address and thoroughly confront the anxieties that accompany blackouts, the government has created a strategy committee. We will act responsibly and provide information, so I am hoping for your understanding; and where the blackouts are concerned, I hope that you will find creative ways to protect your way of life.

This earthquake, tsunami, and the current condition of the nuclear plant can be seen as the worst crisis to have occurred in the sixty-five years that have passed since the war. I think each and every one of us is being asked whether we can overcome this crisis. We have survived severe conditions in the past and created this peaceful and prosperous society. I am confident that with regard to this earthquake and tsunami, the people will all work together to conquer this crisis.

I hope that we can all make the decision to work together, and that while we strengthen our bonds with our families, friends, and communities, we will overcome this crisis and make a new and better country in the process. I appeal to each and every one of you—to every citizen—from my heart. I personally ask this of all of you.

Beginning at 10:22 p.m. I met with Mr. Sengoku, acting leader of the Democratic Party of Japan, Secretary-General Okada, the chairman of the Diet Affairs Committee Jun Azumi, and the chairman of the House of Councillors Azuma Koshiishi to confirm the course of action we would take at a meeting of the secretary-generals of the majority and minority parties scheduled for the following day. The following day was a Monday, so there was a need to determine what to do with regard to Diet deliberations. We, the administration, wanted to limit deliberations as much as possible and call an adjournment in order to focus on the disaster and the nuclear accident. However, at that point in time, the budget had yet to be approved. We hoped to gain its approval and to pass bridging legislation for the extension of a provisional tax-reduction measure, both by the end of March.

The third day ended thus.

March 14 (Monday)

Explosion at the Unit 3 Reactor

Monday arrived and people returned to work. Companies and schools that were not in the disaster-stricken area or in the greater Tokyo metropolitan area went back to life pretty much as usual. Meanwhile, the rolling blackouts in the greater metropolitan area were the cause of a fair amount of confusion.

A little after 9:30 a.m. a meeting of the Emergency Disaster Response Headquarters and the Nuclear Emergency Response Headquarters was held. Beginning before 11 a.m., more precisely at

10:56, I met with Natsuo Yamaguchi of the New Komeito Party. At 11:01 the outer structure of the Unit 3 reactor exploded. Like Unit 1, it was a hydrogen explosion. I learned of the explosion of Unit 3 while in my office with Representative Yamaguchi. My executive secretary came in and turned on the television. It was footage from a camera installed by a local Fukushima television station. Black smoke was billowing directly upward. I was concerned by the color of the smoke. The hydrogen explosion in Unit 1 had produced white smoke, but this time it was black.

The explosion at Unit 3 would come to have an adverse effect on the situation at the adjacent units, 2 and 4. I was made vividly aware of the danger that comes with placing a number of nuclear reactors in close proximity to one another. If a large quantity of radioactive matter was discharged by one reactor, it became difficult to approach not only that reactor but other reactors as well. Furthermore, when a reactor exploded, flying debris might cause damage to adjacent reactors. Placing an emphasis on efficiency, TEPCO had built multiple nuclear reactors on one piece of land and in close proximity to one another. As a result, there were six nuclear reactors at the Fukushima Daiichi Nuclear Power Plant. What would happen if we lost control of all six reactors? What had started out as a vague image of hell was gradually becoming more vivid.

The Unit 3 reactor was different from the other five. It was a thermal reactor that had the capability to use MOX as fuel. While nuclear reactors generally make use of uranium, it was my understanding that MOX fuel is created by mixing uranium with plutonium that has been recovered from used reactor fuel that has been removed and reprocessed. When I met with the Social Democratic Party's representative Mizuho Fukushima the previous day, she had said, "Please be particularly careful because the Unit 3 reactor makes use of MOX fuel."

I asked the related parties to gather immediately. NISA reported that "the reactor containment vessel has not suffered major damage." This was followed by a report that a number of Self-Defense Forces personnel and TEPCO employees who had been performing water-injection work on-site had been injured. Fire trucks and hoses were also damaged, and the water-injection work was aborted. When Unit 3 exploded, pieces of the structure were scattered, and consequently work at the adjacent units 2 and 4 became increasingly difficult as well.

We received fragmentary information regarding conditions on-site but did not know what had caused the explosion. The temperature of the spent fuel pool located at the Unit 4 reactor had been elevated since that morning. Meanwhile, Unit 2 was in a state of emergency.

At 4:24 p.m. I met with Hiroaki Nakanishi, the president of the nuclear reactor manufacturer Hitachi Ltd., and asked for his help. Hitachi had made the Unit 4 reactor that housed the spent fuel pool we were worried about. I had already met with the head of Toshiba and now Hitachi.

As I have stated before, Fukushima Daiichi has six nuclear reactors. The Unit 1 reactor, which began operation in March 1971, was made with the US company General Electric as its general contractor. Thereafter, increasing the role of Japanese manufacturers, Toshiba and GE collaborated on the manufacture of Unit 2 (which began operation in July 1974) and Unit 6 (March 1979). Toshiba independently built Unit 3 (March 1976) and Unit 5 (April 1978). Hitachi built Unit 4, which began operation in October 1978. But even the units that were manufactured by Toshiba and Hitachi had made fundamental use of GE technology. Unit 1 was completely made in the United States. I would later learn that the contract for Unit 1 was what is called a "turnkey contract." As in merely turning the key of a car to start it, this meant that a nuclear power plant had been purchased as an entirely finished product.

These days, people who drive cars learn about a car's general mechanisms in driver's education, but most people drive without an understanding of internal combustion or power transmission. That is why they are unable to repair a car when it breaks down. It may be fine for a privately owned car to be turnkey, but I was shocked to learn that this had been the nature of a contract for a mammoth nuclear power plant. It is my understanding that, generally speaking, when bringing technology from overseas, technicians from abroad work together with Japanese technicians in the building and the testing of the plant. Only when test runs have been successfully accomplished is the transaction complete. But apparently the contract between TEPCO and GE had not been like that. With regard to the Unit 1 reactor, it was built by GE and handed over to TEPCO, who then began its operation. But it had not completely become TEPCO's own technology.

The fact that it had been a turnkey contract was a major hindrance when the accident occurred. It was also a reason TEPCO did not disclose the operation manual to the National Diet of Japan Fukushima Nuclear Accident Independent Investigation Commission after the accident occurred. When it was eventually released, to protect GE's intellectual property rights, some areas had been blacked out.

Crisis at Reactor Unit 2

That evening I continued to receive telephone calls from foreign heads of state. At 5:30 p.m. I spoke with Russia's president Dmitry Medvedev, and at 5:50 p.m. with New Zealand's prime minister John Key. President Medvedev offered humanitarian aid and the supply of energy. In spite of the fact that New Zealand had suffered major earthquakes in September 2010 and February 2011 and were themselves in difficult times, they were offering to help Japan.

After the explosion in the Unit 3 reactor, it became clear that the condition of Unit 2 was grave as well. The pressure was building, and we were unable to inject water. In other words, conditions were such that we were not able to cool the reactor.

To explain simply, the situation with regard to the Unit 2 reactor was similar to units 1 and 3 insofar as the earthquake and tsunami had knocked out its electrical source. However, because workers had succeeded in the manual operation of the reactor core isolation cooling system (RCIC), water injection was possible. For this reason, the venting of Unit 1 was prioritized. But on the afternoon of March 12, with the explosion at Unit 1, the power-supply truck and cables for Unit 2 were damaged and rendered inoperable. What is more, with the explosion at Unit 3 after 11 a.m. on the fourteenth, the exhaust valve on the suppression system was broken and venting was no longer possible. This explosion also damaged the fire trucks and hoses, cutting off the means by which to inject water. The fire truck being used to apply seawater also ran out of gas, and we would learn from later analysis that after 6 p.m. on the fourteenth the spent fuel rods had begun to degenerate.

Being located between units 1 and 3, both of which had exploded, Unit 2 bore the brunt of these explosions. We feared a chain reaction.

When they were having difficulty getting the injection of seawater under way, Special Adviser Hosono had received a phone call from plant manager Yoshida saying, "This may fail." When Hosono told me this, I was speechless. I could only assume that if Yoshida said such a thing, we were probably in a very critical situation.

At 6:22 p.m. the water level in Unit 2 was down 3.7 meters and the spent fuel rods were entirely exposed. At 10:50 p.m. the pressure in Unit 2's reactor containment vessel was climbing unusually high, satisfying the conditions for the declaration of a nuclear emergency in keeping with article 15 of the Nuclear Emergency Preparedness Act.

Units 1 and 3 had already suffered hydrogen explosions. Its cooling system immobilized, the fuel rods in Unit 2 were fully exposed. And the temperature was on the rise in the spent-fuel-rod pool at Unit 4, which had been shut down prior to the accident. A chain reaction had become a reality.

Meanwhile, plant manager Yoshida—who had been discouraged for a time—called Special Adviser Hosono to say, "We still have more fight left in us." Yoshida also reported that when they learned that the fire truck was unable to inject water in Unit 2 because it had run out of gas, the truck was refilled as quickly as possible and they were able to resume the injection of water. When Special Adviser Hosono received this call, I was nearby and asked to have the phone passed to me as well, at which time Yoshida expressed his resolve, saying, "We can still do it." Morale on-site was still high.

March 15 (Tuesday)

Abandonment Is Not an Option

At around 3 a.m. on the fifteenth, when I was napping on the sofa in the room for receiving guests behind my office, I was awoken by my executive secretary. He told me that Minister Kaieda of the Ministry of Economy, Trade, and Industry had arrived. I got up immediately and entered my office. I recall that in addition to Minister Kaieda, Chief Cabinet Secretary Edano, Deputy Chief

Secretary Fukuyama, and special advisers Hosono and Terada were present. The mood was somber. It had been somber ever since the earthquake disaster occurred, but on this occasion the atmosphere was particularly gloomy.

Minister Kaieda said, "TEPCO is proposing a withdrawal from the site of the nuclear accident. What should we do? The nuclear power plant is in a particularly perilous condition." He wasn't saying it outright, but I sensed that he felt there was no other alternative but to abandon the site. I responded, saying, "Do you realize what withdrawal would mean? Units 1, 2, and 3 would all be lost. And then there are the spent fuel pools. If we left everything as is and evacuated the site, not only would Fukushima and Tohoku be done for, but all of eastern Japan. The situation is severe, but there is no choice but to ask them to continue."

According to a report by the National Diet of Japan Fukushima Nuclear Accident Independent Investigation Commission, TEPCO was not considering a "total withdrawal" at this time. This was a misunderstanding on the part of the prime minister's office. I would like to address this matter as follows. With regard to withdrawal, I share in the commission's understanding that the plant manager Yoshida and others on-site were probably prepared to fight to the end. But at TEPCO headquarters at the time, President Shimizu and other members of upper management were discussing the evacuation of most of the Fukushima Daiichi's personnel to Fukushima Daini, as can be seen in the records of TEPCO's video conference calls.

President Shimizu had placed a number of telephone calls to Minister Kaieda and Chief Cabinet Secretary Edano, and in fact, both ministers had acknowledged "the company's intention to withdraw." In my capacity as prime minister, because both ministers had acknowledged the company's intentions, I took action to prevent, at all costs, TEPCO from abandoning the site.

Resolve

The previous evening Minister Kaieda and Chief Cabinet Secretary Edano had turned down TEPCO's requests to evacuate the site, but on the fifteenth, with conditions growing more and more grave, they had apparently begun to think that withdrawal was unavoidable. Then, at about 3 a.m., having decided to solicit the opinion of the prime minister, they called on me.

At this point in time I recognized that if we were unable to contain the nuclear accident, the evacuation zone would probably have to be expanded to include the Tokyo metropolitan area. If that became necessary, the very existence of this country would be in jeopardy. We had to contain the accident, and I believed that we had to be prepared to lose lives in the process.

The notion that "the lives of employees and workers come first" was true under normal conditions. If the workers spent any more time on-site, their exposure to radiation would result in illness and, in some cases, a loss of life. I recognized that conditions were that harsh. But if TEPCO's workers were pulled from the site, large quantities of radioactive material would continue to be disgorged by the uninhabited plant, eventually reaching Tokyo and probably placing TEPCO's own headquarters in the evacuation zone as well.

The horror of a nuclear accident is that time will not take care of it. The more time that passes, the worse it gets. In the case of an accident at a chemical plant, when everything flammable has burned, the fire will go out. But with a nuclear accident there is no extinguishing the flame. And although the hazardous materials given off by a chemical plant may cause significant contamination for a time, this will dissipate in the atmosphere and eventually become harmless. But this is not true of radioactive material. Plutonium has a half-life of 24,000 years.

Abandoning the plant was not an option. No one had asked for it, but we were at war. This was a fight with nuclear reactors, a fight with radiation. An invisible enemy called radiation was attempting to occupy Japan. If we were to temporarily withdraw from the fight and redraw the front lines before returning, radiation levels would only rise in the meantime, making it all the more dangerous to approach the reactors, rendering the problem all the more insurmountable.

In the case of the nuclear accident at Chernobyl, in the Soviet Union, with the military taking the lead, a true "death squad" handled containment and the construction of a stone tomb, a sarcophagus. Thirty people died of acute radiation syndrome, though there are some that say the number was larger. It can be said that the Soviet Union was able to contain the accident because it had a military that followed orders, no questions asked.

Even putting lives on the line to contain the accident, could it truly be contained? Even with the loss of lives, would it still come down to Japan's destruction? It was an even match. This does not mean that the odds of Japan being saved were 50 percent. It means that we would either be saved or we would be destroyed. It was one or the other.

I did not say it out loud, but I had made a decision. I had no choice. I could not just sit there and wait for death to come along. I had no choice but to fight. This enemy had not come from outside. It was something we Japanese had created, and we could not run from it.

When I said, "Abandonment is not an option," Minister Kaieda and the others nodded their assent. Looking then at everyone who had gathered there, I said, "There are still things we can do." Deputy Chief Cabinet Secretary for Crisis Management Itoh said, "We should call on people to persist even if it means the creation of something along the lines of a death squad." Itoh had previously been the chief commissioner of the Metropolitan Police, and he was a pro among pros when it came to crisis management. He seemed to have a good understanding of what would happen to Japan if TEPCO vacated the site. Representatives from NISA and the NSC, who had joined the meeting after it had already begun, also said, "There are still actions to be taken."

I gave orders for President Shimizu of TEPCO to be called immediately. "I am thinking of going to TEPCO headquarters. I want to make a joint command center with members from the government and TEPCO, located at TEPCO headquarters. Special Adviser Hosono will be stationed there."

I had been thinking about the concept of a joint command center since the previous day. At an administrative level it would facilitate a more accurate understanding of the situation on-site and speed up the decision-making process, but, more important, it would make it clear that the government and TEPCO were working together to contain the nuclear accident. At any rate, the information we were receiving was inaccurate and slow to reach us. On-site, TEPCO seemed to have a strong sense of the crisis, but at the company's headquarters there did not seem to be the same sense of urgency. The elected and government officials working in my office believed they were carrying the fate of the country on their backs, while it probably goes without saying that the employees of a private company like TEPCO did not share this way of thinking. That was problematic. We had to change TEPCO's way of seeing things so that they were united with the government in addressing a national crisis.

Beginning immediately after the accident, I conferred often with my staff, from the chief cabinet secretary on down, about how we should handle the events that were unfolding one after another.

But we did not talk about the significance of the accident or about the situation in which our country found itself. We did not talk about such large themes. At a little after 3 a.m. on March 15 I expressed for the first time my understanding that this was a crisis that threatened the very existence of our country.

I didn't want to make a ceremonial speech. We didn't have time for such things. But I did want to share this understanding with those who were present. I cannot clearly remember, but I said something along the lines of "If they withdraw now, all of eastern Japan will be lost. What do we gain by running? We'd probably end up being taken over by another country."

When I said, "We'd probably be taken over," I was not thinking of thieves showing up at a fire. I meant that if we were seen as a country that ran from an accident rather than contain it, there was the possibility that another country would step in and take our place. Running was not an alternative.

A Visit to TEPCO Headquarters

President Shimizu arrived a little after 4 a.m., and when I told him, "Withdrawal is out of the question!" he responded simply with, "Yes, I understand." Rather than request permission to abandon the site, I recall that his immediate capitulation was rather anticlimactic.

I then said, "I want to create a joint command center at TEPCO and to station Special Adviser Hosono there, so please arrange a room and a desk for him." The president agreed to this as well. I then said that I wanted to go to TEPCO headquarters immediately and asked him to make preparations. When I asked how long it would take, he said two hours, but I told him I would go sooner, at 5:30.

I departed my office at 5:26 a.m. I had not left the compound since early on the morning of the twelfth, when I visited the

Fukushima Daiichi Nuclear Power Plant and reviewed the disaster area. Before getting in the car I was surrounded by reporters, so I announced that the government and TEPCO were establishing a joint command center and explained its purpose, saying, "Grave conditions continue, and we want to do whatever we can to overcome this crisis. We want to take command of the situation and see it through."

I arrived at TEPCO headquarters in Uchisaiwaicho a little after 5:30 a.m. Given how slow information had been to reach us, I was surprised at just how close their offices were. Of course, in modern society there isn't much of a correlation between proximity and the speed at which information is transmitted. Just the same, their offices were so close that it seemed it would have been faster to ask a messenger to run memos over.

Their strategic headquarters was on the second floor, and several hundred people were working there. A number of monitors were lined up in the operation room. One of them was connected to Fukushima Daiichi. In other words, there was a system in place to communicate live with Yoshida, the plant manager, and one could get a general sense of the situation at other sites as well. So why wasn't the situation on-site being conveyed to us at the prime minister's offices?

I noted this in the prologue, but it is worth repeating here. I made the following statement to Chairman Katsumata, President Shimizu, and the employees present there.

> More than anyone, you all know the gravity of the situation we are in. There is a need for the government and TEPCO to strategize together, in real time. I will be the director, and Minister Kaieda and President Shimizu will be the deputy directors.
>
> I'm not just concerned about reactor Unit 2. If we abandon reactor Unit 2, what will happen to 1, 3, 4, 5, and 6? And what will

happen to Fukushima Daini? If we withdraw, within months all the reactors and nuclear waste will further deteriorate, resulting in the spread of radiation. It would be two or three times the size of Chernobyl, equal to ten or twenty reactors.

Japan will cease to exist if we don't risk our lives to bring this situation under control. We cannot withdraw quietly and watch from afar. If we were to do that, it would not be out of the question for a foreign country to come along and take our place.

You are all party to this, so I ask you to put your lives on the line. There is nowhere to run. Communication is slow, inaccurate, and often mistaken. Don't become dispirited. Provide the information that is needed. Take in what is happening now, but also look five hours, ten hours, a day, a week ahead, and act accordingly. It doesn't matter how much it costs. No one can do this but TEPCO. When Japan is at risk of failure, withdrawal is out of the question. Mr. Chairman and Mr. President, prepare yourselves. Employees who are over sixty should go to the site. I, too, will work with this resolve. Withdrawal is out of the question. If you withdraw, TEPCO will inevitably fail.

Regarding the circumstances behind the establishment of the joint command center [the Government-TEPCO Integrated Response Office], I said the following at a meeting of the National Diet of Japan Fukushima Nuclear Accident Independent Investigation Commission:

> Generally speaking, the government would not normally march right into the offices or the headquarters of a private company, but if one makes a careful reading of the Nuclear Emergency Preparedness Act, the director-general of the Emergency Disaster Response Headquarters is given the authority to give instructions to the plant operator. It was so written, but I didn't think early on that I could readily exercise this right.
>
> But when the matter of withdrawal came up, I became concerned about discord between TEPCO and the government, and

I felt the need to properly consolidate the decision-making process. It was out of this concern that I proposed the creation of a joint command center and gained the understanding of TEPCO. Thinking back, I certainly could have acted more quickly, but the fact of the matter is that the potential withdrawal provided the impetus, it created the need, for a joint command center. That's what happened.

New Developments

The Government-TEPCO Integrated Response Office was located in TEPCO headquarters. I was its director, but from the start I had no intention of working there. I asked Minister Kaieda and TEPCO's President Shimizu to become deputy directors and Special Adviser Hosono to be the secretariat, and I asked them to be stationed at TEPCO. It would come to pass that Minister Kaieda spent long hours at TEPCO headquarters.

After I had addressed the staff in the operation room, I was led to a meeting room. There was a teleconferencing connection there as well, and it was connected to the Fukushima plant. The system was in place to have a video conference call with the plant's manager, Yoshida, but in no time he said, "I'm sorry, but we are in a state of emergency," and brought the call to a close.

At around 6 a.m. something happened on-site, and things grew tense. Regarding the Unit 2 reactor, an employee at TEPCO headquarters explained to me, "The bottom of the pressure vessel may have been compromised," and "The internal pressure is now the same as the external pressure," and the like.

I thought Unit 2 had exploded, but this was not the case. The structure enclosing Unit 4 had exploded. This, too, was a hydrogen explosion. At the same time, Unit 2's suppression system was damaged and highly radioactive material was released into the atmosphere.

Up until this time, Unit 4 was perceived as safe because it had been idle at the time of the earthquake and tsunami. Since it had been in the middle of periodic tests, all the fuel rods had been removed from the reactor core. But in fact the spent fuel pool was in the greatest danger. Unit 4's fuel rods had been moved into the spent fuel pool that was located adjacent to the reactor. When nuclear fuel rods are inside the reactor, they are encased in both the reactor containment vessel and the pressure vessel, but in the spent fuel pool they were protected only by the structure of the outer building.

In the case of Unit 4, the spent fuel pool is located on the fourth and fifth floors of the structure, but this was much like an ordinary indoor swimming pool and not equipped with any special retaining wall. All is well when the pool is full of water and the cooling system is working, but when cooling is no longer possible, the temperature in the pool rises, the water evaporates, the fuel assemblies are exposed, and they give off radiation. The only thing that keeps this radioactive material from entering the atmosphere is the outer structure.

As a result of the earthquake and tsunami, Unit 4 also suffered from a station blackout and the pool's cooling function was lost. If nothing was done, the water would evaporate and the water level would drop, but calculations suggested conditions would remain stable until March 20, so a priority was placed on handling reactor units 1, 2, and 3. On the previous day, March 14, the temperature of the pool was 84 degrees centigrade, and had not yet reached boiling point [100 degrees centigrade].

So why did it explode at 6:10 a.m. on the fifteenth? TEPCO conjectures that the hydrogen that had accumulated in the Unit 3 reactor had flowed into Unit 4 through shared pipes, resulting in an explosion. At approximately the same time there was a fire in the

Unit 4 reactor as well. Then, concurrent to the explosion in Unit 4, the pressure in Unit 2's suppression system dropped suddenly. None of this information came from on-site, eyewitness reports. It was confirmed by monitors.

Good Fortune

Why had the pressure in Unit 2 dropped so quickly? Most certainly a hole had formed somewhere, allowing steam, gases, and large quantities of radioactive substances to escape. The release of this radioactive material is certainly not excusable, but thanks to this inexplicable hole, a major explosion of the reactor containment vessel was avoided. If one continues to blow up a rubber balloon, it will eventually burst, unable to retain its original form. If, on the other hand, one blows up a paper balloon, at some point the paper's fibers will give way, causing a hole to form and the air to escape. A paper balloon deflates or shrivels up. It doesn't burst. Like a paper balloon, when a hole formed somewhere in reactor Unit 2, the "air" inside was released.

This was neither a part of the Unit 2 design, nor was it accomplished by following a procedure in the manual. No one intentionally opened up a hole as part of a last-resort scheme. Some portion of the structure had probably aged and weakened. When the pressure grew, a hole formed. I am not downplaying the efforts of the workers at the Fukushima Daiichi Nuclear Power Plant or the Self-Defense Forces, the fire department or the police, all of whom were putting their lives on the line, so please do not misunderstand me, but I believe that this nuclear accident did not reach a level causing Japan to collapse because of a convergence of good fortune. One piece of good fortune was the inexplicable drop in pressure in the Unit 2 reactor. If the nuclear reactor in Unit 2 had burst like a rubber balloon, no one would have been able to go anywhere near the area.

Another piece of good fortune was that water remained in the spent-fuel-rod pool in Unit 4. Because the periodic testing of Unit 4 was behind schedule at the time of the accident, the reactor core was full of water. It is thought that for some reason this water flowed into the pool.

We had been saved by good luck. There is no other way to sum it up. But I do not believe we will have such good fortune in the future. Of course, there are ways to prepare in anticipation of a severe accident of this nature. There are manuals, and if we had trained enough, we might have been able to contain the accident and kept it from reaching crisis level. But the fact that we were able to contain it without such preparations—that can only be explained as good luck.

Those who believe that because we were lucky this time, nuclear power plants will be fine in the future are like the members of the Japanese military who thought that because a divine kamikaze wind had saved Japan at the time of the Mongol Invasion [late in the thirteenth century], we could not lose the war in the Pacific.

The release of large quantities of radioactive substances from Unit 2 and the explosion in Unit 4 caused a great deal of anxiety. In particular, it was a matter of grave concern that the quantities of radioactive substances released were the greatest to date. We would have to consider expanding the evacuation area.

An Appeal to the People

March 15 was a Tuesday. There was a regularly scheduled cabinet meeting, so I returned to the prime minister's compound a little after 8:30 a.m. I had been at TEPCO headquarters for a bit less than three hours. Although I had created the Integrated Response Office and made myself its director, I had no intention of being stationed at TEPCO or taking command. But in my capacity as director it was important that I spend even a few hours sitting in TEPCO headquarters. Thereafter, even if I was not present, I could have the authority vested in me transferred to the secretariat, to Special Adviser Hosono, who took command of the situation.

Because I also had to prepare for the cabinet meeting, I left a little after 8:30, while Minister Kaieda and special advisers Hosono and Terada remained and turned to the work of setting up the Integrated Response Office.

Generally speaking, the chief cabinet secretary held two press conferences per day, conveying necessary information regarding earthquake and tsunami damage and conditions at the nuclear power plant to the general public. On this day, with the explosion at Unit 4 and the reduction in pressure at Unit 2, given an increase in the danger, people living between twenty and thirty kilometers of the Fukushima Daiichi Nuclear Power Plant were asked to remain indoors at all times. In keeping with this, I held a press conference at 11 a.m., and below I have included a record of my appeal to the people.

> I want to inform you, the people of Japan, with regard to the situation at the Fukushima nuclear power plants. I urge you to listen calmly to this information.
>
> As has been explained previously, the earthquake and tsunami caused the reactors at the Fukushima Daiichi Nuclear Power Plant to shut down, and none of the diesel engines that would normally have provided emergency power to the cooling systems are functioning, so we have been using every means at our disposal to cool the nuclear reactors. However, with the buildup of hydrogen and the hydrogen explosions at the Unit 1 and Unit 3

reactors, and a fire in the Unit 4 reactor, the concentration of radioactivity being leaked into the vicinity of the plant has risen considerably. And there is a heightened risk of the further leakage of radioactive material.

Most residents have already been evacuated to a distance of more than twenty kilometers from the Fukushima Daiichi Nuclear Power Plant, but I want to reiterate that we need to ask everyone who is living within the area to evacuate to a location outside the area at this time.

Moreover, in view of the developing situation, those of you who are outside the twenty-kilometer radius but still within a thirty-kilometer radius, I ask that you remain inside your homes, offices, or other structures. Further, with regard to the Fukushima Daini Nuclear Power Plant, most people have already evacuated beyond a ten-kilometer radius, but we are asking everyone who remains within that area to evacuate now.

We are presently doing everything possible to prevent further explosions and the leakage of radioactive material. At this moment, TEPCO's workers and other related personnel are taking great personal risks in their tireless efforts to supply water to the reactors. I realize that you, the people of Japan, are greatly concerned about the situation, but I sincerely urge everyone to act in a calm manner, bearing in mind the tremendous efforts under way to prevent further radiation leaks.

I ask this of all of you, the people of Japan.

On this occasion I took only one question from a reporter, who asked, "Excuse me, Prime Minister, but you made no reference to the Unit 2 reactor. Isn't it in an increasingly grave condition?" I responded, "As I have just stated, conditions vary depending on the reactor unit, and we are taking action with an eye to the overall picture. With regard to an explanation of the condition of individual reactors, it is my understanding that there may be a separate report from TEPCO."

As the executive in chief, that was all I could say at that point in time. I would not hide anything that had happened, but as the prime minister I would also not say anything of which I could not be certain. That was my policy. This was my first experience of a severe accident of this sort, and no one could predict the future with any confidence. According to law, the NSC and NISA could advise the prime minister, but these organizations were not capable of making any assertions. I was able to get second opinions from my network at the Tokyo Institute of Technology, but their opinions only offered a point of reference. Some said that it might mean the end of eastern Japan, while others suggested it would not become a major problem. It would have been irresponsible for the government to release all those opinions and ask individual citizens to judge for themselves and take actions as they saw fit.

This is not the meaning of "making information available to the public." The government has to be ready to take responsibility for the information it officially releases. Information for which the government cannot take responsibility cannot be released. That is one difference between the government and the press. Of course, I do not believe the press should be allowed to spread information without taking any responsibility for it either, but the weight of responsibility is different for the press and the government.

In particular, with regard to statements made by the prime minister at press conferences, insofar as they are the definitive words of the country's representative they are extremely weighty. They cannot be revised and they cannot be withdrawn. It is there, walking that fine line where it is most difficult to make a judgment, that press conferences are held.

I would like to make a note here regarding the fact that the prime minister's office did not make use of SPEEDI data. [SPEEDI is the "System for Prediction of Environmental Emergency Dose

Information," which is designed to predict the flow of radioactive substances.] It is true that this data was conveyed to the offices of the prime minister, which is to say it reached someone in the building or someone in the organization, but it did not reach me. I and my staff did not see it and choose not to make use of it, nor is it true that we hid it. This was a problem involving the transmission of information within the government, and as the chief executive I cannot excuse myself from responsibility for it, but I do want to go on record saying that the elected officials and staff working at the prime minister's office did not intentionally conceal this information.

Selling Japan

Establishing the Government-TEPCO Integrated Response Office at TEPCO's main office and arranging for Special Adviser Hosono to be stationed there improved our communication greatly, but that alone would not result in better conditions at the site of the nuclear accident. The crisis continued.

It was confirmed at 12:25 p.m. that the fire at the Unit 4 reactor had burned out. But the roof over the spent fuel pool had been blown off by the explosion. With nothing overhead, the water would evaporate and radioactive substances would enter the atmosphere. We had to replenish water at all costs. On the other hand, the same could be said for units 1 and 3. The absence of a roof on Unit 4 could be seen as a plus because it was possible to add water from the air. For this reason we also began to consider pouring water from the Self-Defense Forces' helicopters on all the spent fuel pools.

Early on the morning of the fifteenth, with conditions at the nuclear power plant growing worse, there was a rapid sell-off of Japanese stocks at the Tokyo Stock Exchange and the market dropped significantly. Foreign embassies had begun to advise their citizens to evacuate. I would learn later that many of the musicians scheduled to perform in Japan canceled their tours. But I also heard that some musicians came to Japan as a show of support, and for that I am grateful.

All that said, conditions were beginning to portend the worst-case scenario, the evacuation of 50 million people. And evacuation alone would not be enough. Nuclear catastrophes spread to the economy, the society, the culture, every imaginable area.

Going on the Offensive

With the creation of the Integrated Response Office, TEPCO and the government began to strategize together in earnest, as one. This began with the use of Self-Defense Forces' helicopters to airlift water and pour it on the spent fuel pools.

Before 4 p.m. on the fifteenth, Defense Minister Kitazawa brought Chief of Staff Ryoichi Oriki to the prime minister's offices to discuss the application of water. Chief of Staff Oriki said, "The Self-Defense Forces' mission is to protect the lives of the people. If so commanded, we will do everything in our power." Those were heartening words.

It goes without saying that we wanted TEPCO to do everything they could. Having established a joint command center, the government not only wanted to be better informed, we wanted to be able to take part even more aggressively in containing the nuclear accident. I spoke with Defense Minister Kitazawa of the importance of the Self-Defense Forces' role.

In the evening, Special Adviser Hosono, who had become the secretariat of the Integrated Response Office, came to report to me, telling me of everything that had happened after I had left

TEPCO that morning. I imagined that it was not easy to represent the government while surrounded by TEPCO's employees, but I trusted that if anyone could do it, he could. And performing in my stead, Special Adviser Hosono exercised his duties well.

As with the arrangement of power-supply trucks on the night of March 11, almost everything ran more smoothly with the help of the police and the Self-Defense Forces. But if every single matter had to pass through NISA or METI before it got to us, and we then had to make arrangements with the related government departments, it took too much time. After stationing Special Adviser Hosono at TEPCO's Integrated Response Office, he was able to work directly with the related ministries and agencies. I have been told that operations became quite smooth thereafter.

A number of government staff were placed at Secretariat Hosono's disposal. One among them was Hiroshi Ikukawa, who had been my executive secretary when I served as deputy prime minister and minister of state for science and technology policy. At the time of the earthquake he had been on assignment from the Ministry of Education, Culture, Sports, Science, and Technology [MEXT] to RIKEN Institute of Chemical and Physical Research. At my request he was stationed at TEPCO as a member of our staff. He reported the situation to me on-site several times a day, every day of the week, for the following six months without missing a single day. In this way I was able to have a real-time sense of what was happening, and this helped me a great deal when making decisions.

March 16 (Wednesday)

Instructions to the Self-Defense Forces

The Fukushima Daiichi Nuclear Power Plant remained in a state of crisis. Fire was confirmed coming from the structure

enclosing the Unit 4 reactor at 5:45 a.m. It was in the same location where a fire had occurred the day before. At 8:37 a.m., white
smoke was seen coming from Unit 3. It was feared that the water
in the spent fuel pool had come to a boil. At this rate the pool in
Unit 4 could be expected to come to a boil as well. The hourly
quantity of radiation at the plant's gate was measured at ten milli-
sieverts at 10:40 a.m.

There was nothing we could do but keep cooling the spent fuel
assemblies and the reactors, to continue applying water. It may be
a strange way of putting it, but given the hydrogen explosions and
the appearance of holes for reasons unknown, and given that the
reactors were no longer of any use, while conditions were certainly
grave, the action to be taken had become quite simple. Keep everything cool.

Of course, I knew that adding water to cool things down was
easier said than done. More than anything, high radiation levels
made it difficult to approach the reactors, and the area was also
strewn with rubble from the earthquake, tsunami, and repeated
explosions. It was the worst possible work environment, and in
that environment we were fighting against time.

In a meeting that began at 12:46 that afternoon, I conferred with
Defense Minister Kitazawa, the administrative vice-minister of
defense Kimito Nakae, director of the Defense Intelligence Headquarters Koji Shimohira, and Special Adviser Hosono. I asked
them to consider having the Self-Defense Forces take more of a
leadership role in the containment of the nuclear accident, rather
than the logistical support they had provided to date. As a country,
we had to devote all our energies to the containment of this
accident.

At around 4 p.m., a Self-Defense Forces helicopter took off with
the intention of dropping water on the reactor from the air, but

when they approached Unit 3, radiation levels were so high that they were unable to perform the task. Of course they had to be directly above the reactor to make a drop, and radiation levels were highest there. On this day, they were unable to flood the reactor, but they were accompanied by TEPCO personnel who took a video of units 3 and 4 and were able to visually confirm that there was water in the spent fuel pool in Unit 4.

I told Defense Minister Kitazawa, "It is certainly a difficult task, but I hope you can find a way to accomplish it tomorrow." The following day the strategy of applying water by helicopter would meet with success.

I talked on the telephone with Ban Ki-moon, the secretary-general of the United Nations, beginning at 10:16 p.m. He expressed his sympathies regarding the earthquake and tsunami, and told me he was moved by the Japanese people's efforts to overcome this national crisis. I thanked him for these sentiments.

He also told me, "With regard to the nuclear accident at Fukushima, the United Nations will not spare any expense in supporting Japan." And, "The United Nations stands with the Japanese people." With regard to the nuclear accident, I said, "Japan will provide the necessary information to the international community."

It was as could be expected, but I was reminded that the world was watching Fukushima.

March 17 (Thursday)

Dousing the Plant

At 9:48 a.m., two Self-Defense Forces helicopters poured water on the Unit 3 reactor from above, and again at fifty-two and fifty-eight minutes after the hour, and at 10 a.m., for a total of four times. This was shown live on television, and I watched, praying for their success.

This strategy, which had been put off the previous day because of high radiation levels, finally met with success. For the Self-Defense Forces personnel this was truly life-threatening work, and they attached metal plates to the helicopters in an effort to block any radiation.

From the early stages of this nuclear accident, the Self-Defense Forces had been gathering information. After 7 p.m. on March 11, after a state of emergency was declared, Defense Minister Kitazawa issued an order for a nuclear-disaster relief operation and the Central Nuclear Biological Chemical Weapon Defense Unit (CNBC), which is part of the Central Readiness Force (CRF), headed for Fukushima. This unit is trained to handle nuclear, biological, and chemical weapons. Although they had not been trained with a nuclear accident in mind, they were the unit in the Self-Defense Forces that was best equipped for a nuclear accident. As I described previously, on the night of the eleventh, when the staff of the prime minister's office was working to get power-supply trucks to Fukushima, they were greatly helped by the Self-Defense Forces. And when CNBC was working on-site to replenish the coolant, Unit 3 exploded, injuring some members of the unit.

Although the Self-Defense Forces had been mobilized since shortly after the accident, their support had been mainly logistical. Now, having been asked to take more of a leadership role, and with the establishment of the Integrated Response Office and smoother communication with the site, it became easier for the Self-Defense Forces to act and to carry out strategic work. Accomplishing the flooding of the reactors was the first step in turning things around, and going on the offensive as we tried to limit the spread of this accident.

In addition to the introduction of water by helicopters, the Self-Defense Forces, fire department, and police began to spray water on the spent fuel pools from the ground. The government and TEPCO's all-out collaborative effort to contain the accident had begun.

At 10:22 a.m., immediately after succeeding with this strategy, I had a telephone conversation with President Obama. He had also been watching the Self-Defense Forces' flooding operation on television and had been impressed. This effort was a highly visible strategy carried out with the knowledge that there was a potential for life-threatening levels of radiation. The US Army apparently understood this danger more than anyone else. I was told by Defense Minister Kitazawa that after witnessing this undertaking, the US military's attitude changed radically. Members of the US military who were here in Japan to help with the earthquake and tsunami relief effort as part of Operation Tomodachi were also worried about the nuclear accident. I was told that they had been uncertain as to how serious the Japanese government was about resolving this problem, but the Self-Defense Forces' actions had shown them our commitment.

My telephone conversation with President Obama lasted for more than thirty minutes. This was my second conversation with President Obama since the earthquake; this time our talk was very concrete. The president told me, "In addition to the present assistance by the US military and the work of rescue teams, we are prepared to provide nuclear experts and any manner of other aid toward middle- and long-term reconstruction." President Obama was fully aware of the extremely grave condition of the Fukushima Daiichi Nuclear Power Plant and seemed to be concerned that Japan's "bureaucratic handling" of incoming aid might be impairing it.

After expressing my gratitude for the United States' support, I explained, "We are doing everything in our power to address the nuclear accident, mobilizing every organization, the police and the Self-Defense Forces included. With regard to the support you are offering, we would like to discuss this with US representatives and to continue close contact between US and Japanese nuclear experts."

Finally, we promised to openly share any information we might have. There is a ceremonial element to talks between heads of state, but deeper matters are also discussed. In this conversation I was assured of even more support handling the nuclear accident.

Asking the Governor of Tokyo for Help

A plenary session of the House of Representatives was held at 1 p.m. It was the first plenary session since the earthquake, and it began with a moment of silent prayer. Immediately after the prayer I returned to my office and met with Defense Minister Kitazawa and the leaders of the Defense Ministry to express my appreciation for the seawater-dumping operation.

The Self-Defense Forces alone were not enough. We needed to ask the firefighters, riot police, and others for their help applying water as well. Among the firefighters, the city of Tokyo had the most advanced heavy equipment. At around 7 p.m. I called the parliamentary secretary for the cabinet office Yukihiko Akutsu. Prior to becoming a Diet member, Mr. Akutsu had been private secretary to Tokyo's governor[6] Shintaro Ishihara back when he was a member of the House of Representatives. I did not know if the two of them remained close, but wanting to reach Governor Ishihara as quickly as possible, I asked Mr. Akutsu for his help. At this time Mr. Akutsu was in Miyagi Prefecture as acting chair of the on-site operational headquarters for the Headquarters for Emergency Disaster Control. I told him, "We need to flood the spent-fuel-rod pools, and we need the Tokyo Metropolitan Fire Department's most advanced fire trucks. Can you ask Mr. Ishihara?"

Mr. Akutsu contacted Mr. Ishihara immediately, and I received a call back from him saying that the governor was at home and giving me the number. When I called and asked for Mr. Ishihara's cooperation, he readily consented.

In fact we had done something regrettable to the Tokyo Fire Department. On March 16 TEPCO had asked to borrow a special disaster rescue truck from the Tokyo Fire Department. The Fire and Disaster Management Agency had arranged for the fire department to transport the vehicle. A TEPCO employee would then drive it on-site. But when the Tokyo Fire Department brought the truck to Iwaki City in Fukushima Prefecture, no one was there to collect it. When a TEPCO employee did finally come, they did not appear to understand what was going on, so the fire department was forced to return. So we had essentially trampled on the Tokyo Fire Department's goodwill. I was not familiar with these circumstances when, on the seventeenth, I asked Governor Ishihara for his help.

Governor Ishihara and I see many things differently, and I know he is usually critical of me and the Democratic Party of Japan, but in the face of a national crisis he looked beyond those differences and cooperated. When I learned after the fact that equipment that had been taken to the vicinity of the site was forced to return because of poor communication on our part, I was all the more grateful. I understand that Governor Ishihara's cooperation was not for me personally, but for Japan, and that is fine.

When the Tokyo Fire Department's rescue unit put their lives on the line, fire departments from other prefectures followed suit.

The employees of TEPCO were also risking their lives on-site. The earthquake and nuclear disaster were a reminder to me of Japan's on-site skills.

To the Imperial Palace

On March 17 we also attended to personnel matters. I was told that the seventy-eight-year-old deputy chief cabinet secretary Hirohisa Fujii wanted to retire because of his advanced age, and I decided to replace him with Yoshito Sengoku, the acting president of the Democratic Party of Japan. Mr. Sengoku had supported me as the chief cabinet secretary when I became prime minister, but had been working outside the cabinet as acting representative of the party since a reshuffling in January. Given his familiarity with the bureaucracy, he was being asked to work on this crisis. Only a few months before, Mr. Sengoku had been chief, and now, as deputy chief, he would be working for Mr. Edano, who was younger than he was. While this could be seen as a demotion, he readily accepted the position.

According to law, the position of deputy chief cabinet secretary is an appointment requiring confirmation by the emperor. Toward this end, it was necessary to perform an attestation ceremony at the Imperial Palace. Protocol determined that men were to dress in morning wear. But the circumstances being what they were, after discussing the matter with the Imperial Household Agency, it was determined that I could attend wearing a suit.

I arrived at the Imperial Palace at 7:55 p.m. and attended the attestation ceremony in my suit. His Majesty the Emperor wore a suit as well. Apparently this was the first time an attestation ceremony had been conducted in informal attire.

At this point the nuclear accident was still in a crisis state. If we were unable to contain it, I was thinking about particular aspects of the worst-case scenario, such as the timing of the removal of the imperial family from Tokyo. As prime minister, this was a matter of course.

Meanwhile, I asked Mr. Fujii to stay on as a special adviser. As the number of special advisers is set at five, I unfortunately had to ask Koichi Kato to step down. I returned to my offices at 8:48 p.m. and gave notice of my appointment of Mr. Fujii as special adviser (because special advisers to the prime minister are not subject to the emperor's approval).

After 11 p.m., Special Adviser Hosono came to report to me from the Integrated Response Office at TEPCO. He told me that after the Self-Defense Forces' helicopter's success applying water that morning, the Metropolitan Police Department's high-pressure water trucks and an additional five Self-Defense Forces high-pressure fire trucks had sprayed water from ground level in the afternoon.

I instructed him to keep on flooding and cooling the plant since that was all we could do.

March 18 (Friday)

One Week Passed

On this day, TEPCO finally announced that there were a total of 4,546 spent fuel assemblies in the spent fuel pools adjacent to the Fukushima Daiichi Nuclear Power Plant's six reactors. Of this number, 1,331 were located beside reactor Unit 4.

At 2:15 p.m., I received a courtesy call from Yukiya Amano, director general of the International Atomic Energy Agency (IAEA). He conveyed a message from the international community, saying, "We want to assist you in handling the accident at the nuclear power plant." To this I responded, "We are doing everything in our power with regard to the plant. We will provide information to IAEA and the international community with the utmost transparency."

At 7 p.m. I spoke on the telephone with President Sarkozy of France. He said, "If there is anything you need, please tell me." After thanking him for his sympathy, his expression of solidarity, and his offer of aid, I told him what we were doing for victims of the disaster and about conditions at the Fukushima nuclear power plants.

One week had passed since the earthquake struck. At this juncture, in my capacity as prime minister, I wanted to address the people directly and in my own words, so I held a press conference beginning at 8:13 p.m. I spoke of the two crises we faced, caused by the earthquake and tsunami and the nuclear accident. I stated frankly that, with regard to the nuclear accident, conditions were such that any diversion was unacceptable. I also expressed my heartfelt sympathy for all those living in shelters.

Even now, I am filled with feelings of regret that many people are still living in shelters, and that members of the same family have been forced to live apart.

I have reproduced here most of what I said in my one-week address:

> We are now facing two large problems. In addition to the damage caused by a massive earthquake and tsunami, a major nuclear accident was brought on by the earthquake and tsunami. We are confronted by both crises.
>
> Our relief work has been conducted in the midst of a great deal of confusion, and there have been many hurdles to cross. We are gradually overcoming these difficulties, however, and relief supplies will begin to reach those who are suffering and in need of them. I also believe we will start to move forward, though slowly, in reconstructing people's lives. With respect to Japan's recovery, I am

confident that the nation as a whole will overcome the damage of the earthquake and tsunami.

Meanwhile, the situation with the nuclear power accident in Fukushima remains precarious. At this moment, all the people involved from TEPCO, the Self-Defense Forces, and the police and fire departments are literally risking their lives to overcome this crisis. I, too, am prepared to do whatever it takes to resolve this nuclear accident. With the help of the Japanese people, on-site and elsewhere, I am committed to moving beyond this crisis and restoring our peace of mind. With this conviction in my heart, I will work even harder from this day forward.

We have received a truly great number of messages of consolation and support from countries around the world. Thus far, we have received offers of support from 117 countries and regions and from twenty-nine international organizations, and relief activities are already under way. I am extremely grateful.

Facing the largest crisis in our country's history since World War II, but with the support of the entire world, we must not be despondent. Each and every one of us must hold a strong resolve in our hearts that we will do whatever it takes to overcome this crisis and move forward together.

To everyone living in the evacuation shelters, I express my heartfelt sympathies for your hardships, in the cold, with inadequate supplies of food and water, and limited access to toilet facilities. I ask that you help one another, that you work together with your families and communities and even with the complete strangers living beside you to endure the hardships of life in an evacuation shelter.

The following is a record of the subsequent Q&A with members of the media:

Question: My name is Aoyama. I'm with Nippon TV. With regard to the Fukushima Daiichi Nuclear Power Plant, I believe this accident is causing considerable concern not only to those living in the surrounding area, but to the people of Japan. Furthermore, in some quarters there is growing distrust of the information being released by the government. In your capacity as Japan's prime minister, how dangerous would you say the current situation is? Or, alternatively, to what extent should we feel at ease? And what do you think lies ahead? Please tell us these things, using as many concrete examples as you can.

My Answer: The chief cabinet secretary and I have released everything we know about the ongoing accident at the nuclear power plant. I want to say this again to the people of Japan and to the global community as a whole. That said, conditions at the Fukushima nuclear power plant are such that a loss of focus is not permissible. I am being candid in this regard. Right now, TEPCO, the Self-Defense Forces, firefighters, the police and other personnel are working on our behalf, ready to make the ultimate sacrifice, to resolve this situation. Today we sprayed water on the Unit 3 reactor. While conditions are such that we must remain vigilant, by taking such actions we should be able to bring the situation firmly under control and extract ourselves from the present situation in the not-too-distant future. I want the people of Japan to know that we are doing everything in our power to move things in that direction.

Question: I'm Igarashi, with *Yomiuri Shimbun* [newspaper]. Mr. Prime Minister, as you have said, the earthquake and tsunami were followed by the accident at the nuclear power plant and the blackouts. And most important, there is the matter of the relief of the disaster victims. Any one of these would be a serious crisis, and we are faced with a whole chain of them. In that context, many people are concerned whether the present government's response has been sufficient. Do you feel that the government's current approach is adequate? Today, Secretary-General Okada [of the Democratic Party of Japan] suggested there was a need to increase the number of ministers in your cabinet by three. Can you tell us if you have any concrete plans to strengthen the government's disaster response?

My Answer: The government moved swiftly to take action immediately after the earthquake struck, and since then has been doing everything in its power to resolve these problems and overcome the crisis. Building on this, to further bolster the disaster-response network, the ruling and opposition parties are presently discussing ways to strengthen the cabinet. Through these and other efforts, I intend to further improve our strength and adaptability in responding to this crisis.

Question: I'm Tanaka, with *Mainichi Shimbun* [newspaper]. I have a question regarding reconstruction in the disaster-struck regions. In your statement just now, you spoke of doing everything you can to prepare an environment in which people can live without anxiety, and of asking people to move to new locations. The areas affected by this disaster have seen tremendous damage, with local government buildings totally washed away so reconstruction of the infrastructure is going to take a considerable amount of time. What plans do you have for the people currently living in evacuation shelters during this reconstruction period? I would appreciate if you could tell me what the government is currently considering in this regard.

My Answer: In the face of a lengthy evacuation period, we have had a variety of offers, and we are preparing a number of measures to address the situation. We have received offers from all around the country to take in evacuees. Offers have come from local governments, from various organizations, and even from individuals. And we are soliciting offers from our side as well. To prevent people from having to live in difficult evacuation conditions for a long time, the government will be doing all it can to help people around the country provide places for the disaster victims to live. This is what we are thinking.

We had a mountain of problems.

Going Home

This night, at 9:47 p.m., I returned home to my official residence for the first time in one week. When I learned that as long as I remained in the office, my staff would not be able to return home, I decided to go home. Everyone was working frantically.

There was truly no time for rest or sleep. During the past week the only occasions on which I left my office were to visit Fukushima Daiichi and the disaster-stricken areas early on the morning of the twelfth, to go to TEPCO headquarters early on the morning of the fifteenth, to attend a plenary session of the House of Representatives at the Diet on the seventeenth, and to attend an attestation ceremony at the Imperial Palace that same night. Just those four times.

After March 19

The Danger Continues

After March 19, we had by no means extricated ourselves from the crisis we were in. In particular, an explosion in Unit 4 had destroyed the walls of the outer structure. The building's columns were the only thing holding it together. If a large aftershock caused the structure to collapse, the spent fuel assemblies would spill out. If this occurred, it would be out of our hands. We hurriedly performed reconstruction work and could only pray that a large aftershock would not come in the meantime.

TEPCO was working hard to restore external electric power to Fukushima Daiichi. On the nineteenth, when I was told that it would be restored I was quite relieved. I thought that the restoration of electricity meant that cooling systems would begin to function. But that was wishful thinking. Even with the restoration of electricity, because the pumps and other equipment that circulated the cooling water were broken, the cooling system did not function. We had no choice but to continue flooding the plant with water from the outside. Until we could set up provisional pumps, we would continue applying water using fire trucks and water cannons.

With regard to the application of water, the Tokyo Fire Department's Hyper Rescue Team also put their lives on the line. And fire departments from other prefectures helped out in what became a nationwide effort to contain the nuclear accident. Because this was a collaborative effort involving multiple organizations—police, fire, and Self-Defense Forces personnel from all over, in addition to TEPCO's construction crew—the chain of command became an issue.

As the head of the Government-TEPCO Integrated Response Office, Special Adviser Hosono encamped himself at TEPCO and, after evaluating conditions there, he determined that it would be best for the Self-Defense Forces to be given responsibility for the comprehensive coordination of efforts on-site. On the eighteenth, Minister Kaieda and Special Adviser Hosono issued "Instructions," and these were reissued on the twentieth in my name. The instructions stated, "The Self-Defense Forces will play a pivotal role regarding implementation on-site, and after coordinating the efforts of related government agencies and TEPCO, they will make final decisions" regarding the discharge of water and the like. The instructions also specified that "the Self-Defense Forces would handle the integrated management of the on-site coordination point at J-Village."

With the establishment of the Integrated Response Office, it had become possible for government agencies and TEPCO to work in concert with one another. Furthermore, the Integrated Response Office and Special Adviser Hosono's network of ministries and government offices facilitated the coordination of efforts by the Self-Defense Forces and the police and fire departments.

This also became possible because the heads of the police and fire departments recognized that when it came to a national disaster, there was no alternative but to operate with the Self-Defense

Forces at the helm. Actually, this was the first time the police and fire departments worked subordinate to the Self-Defense Forces, and there were no legal precedents for the collaboration of these organizations. More than anything we were in a race against time, and because it involved a limited geographical area, we were able to draw up instructions of this nature. Of course the matter was debated, but there was no sense of hesitation. The crisis was so great that it could not be contained without the Self-Defense Forces taking on this role.

Repercussions

It was not until late April that we thought we had escaped the danger of the nuclear accident spreading further. On April 17, TEPCO released "A Roadmap for the Containment of the Accident at the Fukushima Daiichi Nuclear Power Plant." This document suggested "there is a steady trend toward a reduction in radiation levels." A goal of three months was set for the achievement of step 1, namely "the stabilization of the cooling of the nuclear reactors and the establishment of a place to store contaminated water." The document went on to say, "Radiation leakage is under control, and radiation levels have been largely suppressed." Step 2 was to "maintain steady cooling and reduce the quantity of contaminated water." This was to be achieved three to six months after the completion of step 1.

In the "Roadmap" there were five items in three categories that needed immediate attention. The first category was "cooling," and it included the cooling of the nuclear reactors and the cooling of the spent-fuel-rod pools. The second category was "suppression." It involved the containment, storage, treatment, and reuse of retained water contaminated with radioactive materials and similarly the suppression of radioactive materials in the atmosphere and the soil. The third category, "monitoring and decontamination," was the monitoring, reduction, and publication of radiation levels in the three evacuation zones (the forced evacuation zone, the voluntary evacuation zone, and the zone prepared for evacuation in case of an emergency). TEPCO alone had this many issues to address. Because this roadmap was limited to the containment of the accident, there was no mention here of reparations.

One month later, on May 17, TEPCO published a progress report vis-à-vis the roadmap. The report stated that there had been no change in the schedule for the achievement of the goals in the first two categories. If all went according to plan, the consistent cooling of the nuclear reactors would become possible in July, and the containment and reduction of contaminated water would be achieved between October 2011 and January 2012.

Accepting this, the government, at a meeting of the Nuclear Emergency Response Headquarters, decided on a "Roadmap for Immediate Actions for the Assistance of Residents Affected by the Nuclear Accident." This involved a detailed follow-up by all the government ministries toward the improvement of the lives of the evacuees, temporary housing, jobs, the education of children, additional extended evacuations, the handling of farm animals, and so on.

As a result of the accident, high radiation levels were being measured in quite a wide area. People were anxious about hazards to their health and the contamination of food, and the government was also busy addressing these issues. There was also the problem of processing contaminated debris.

And the need to address TEPCO's own fiscal crisis came to the surface. Furthermore, there was the problem of whether to make TEPCO pay compensation for damages. Regardless, there was the need for a huge amount of capital. Even if we were to pay this out of the national treasury, how should that be handled? And we had to think about how to address the demand for electricity in the summer.

In addition to the problem of restoration and recovery from the earthquake and tsunami, we could not neglect domestic affairs and diplomacy either. The national government's problems were piling up.

Hard Work

On July 19, the Nuclear Emergency Response Headquarters reported that the circulating injection cooling system was operating, the cooling systems had stabilized, and the quantity of radioactive matter being released was reduced to 0.0000005 of what it had been immediately after the accident. Step 1 on the roadmap had been accomplished. More than anything, this was thanks to a concerted containment effort on-site, on the front lines of a nuclear accident, and on the part of the plant manager Yoshida, and the employees of TEPCO and of other related firms.

Also in July, I made my second visit to J-Village. While there, I met people working on-site, and I had the opportunity to express my gratitude directly, saying, "It is thanks to your selfless devotion that we have achieved this degree of control over the reactors. I offer my heartfelt thanks. I believe that your efforts are saving Japan." I continue to have these feelings for the people on-site. I would like to express my high esteem for those who continue to this day to work hard and risk their lives at the site of a nuclear accident.

2

Taking Action before Stepping Down

Even when there was no longer a need for an emergency response to the nuclear accident, a pile of problems remained. In order to have a renewed understanding of the damage caused by the earthquake and tsunami and of the condition of those who had been evacuated because of the nuclear accident, I visited the disaster-stricken area and several shelters and temporary housing sites. Where the earthquake and tsunami had struck, the coastal areas had been washed away. It was taking time to dispose of the rubble, to build temporary housing, and to rebuild fishing ports, towns, and private homes, but the recovery and reconstruction work were progressing gradually.

During my visits I had the opportunity to listen to people who had evacuated from Fukushima. One woman who had lived near the nuclear power plant spoke with tears in her eyes, "My husband is an employee of TEPCO and he is working at the Fukushima nuclear power plant. For that reason, I am looked at it with a critical eye even though my husband is working on-site and well aware of the danger involved." And when another man told me, "My house is farther away than America," I was at a loss for words. While the suffering of those who were displaced by the earthquake and tsunami is certainly great, I acutely felt the psychological weight of being unable to return to a home that, while physically unscathed, had been rendered uninhabitable by the nuclear accident.

And I heard talk of children being bullied at shelters. I keenly felt that the nuclear accident had deeply scarred a large number of people. This awareness of human suffering was at the heart of all my remaining efforts as prime minister of Japan.

Partisan Politics

At a meeting immediately following the earthquake, the heads of Japan's ruling and opposition parties pledged their full support in the face of this unprecedented calamity. Unfortunately, however, there was little change in the LDP's efforts to topple the Democratic Party's government at the earliest possible date.

In the face of this national crisis, I felt the need for a nonpartisan cabinet. In particular, with the opposition party having a majority in the House of Councillors, there was an urgent need for a coalition with the Liberal Democratic Party. With this in mind, I lobbied for a one-on-one meeting with Sadakazu Tanigaki, president of the LDP. Because I was not particularly close to him, I asked the representative Koichi Kato, the original leader of the Tanigaki faction, to mediate on my behalf. Representative Kato and I had worked together across party lines and developed a relationship of trust at the time of the LDP and Socialist Party coalition government back in 1994 and in responding to more recent financial crises. Representative Kato appealed to President Tanigaki repeatedly on my behalf, but the LDP had lost a large number of seats in the 2009 elections. Rather than participate in a nonpartisan cabinet devoted to national salvation, a large number of LDP representatives were pursuing political gains. They wanted to oust the Democratic Party government as soon as possible. It was such individuals who worked to prevent me from meeting with President Tanigaki alone. As a result I was neither able to meet with him alone nor to realize the creation of a coalition cabinet.

In the aftermath of the earthquake disaster, in keeping with a radical increase in the quantity of work required of the cabinet, I also wanted to increase the number of Cabinet ministers and aides, but the LDP was opposed for fear it would strengthen the Democratic Party's position. Furthermore, there had been repeated criticisms of my administration's handling of the nuclear accident. We were accused of providing false information. On June 2, a mere three months after the disaster, the LDP made a parliamentary motion of no confidence against my cabinet as their relentless effort to overthrow my government continued. When responding to an earthquake and a nuclear disaster, there should be a one-year moratorium on interparty fighting and national unity when addressing the matters at hand. I am in part responsible for this not coming to pass, but it was also the unfortunate outcome of an emphasis on partisan politics.

Groundwater

After establishing the Government-TEPCO Integrated Response Office on March 15, a large number of problems began to accumulate around Secretariat Hosono. It was for this reason that when he requested the assistance of Sumio Mabuchi I appointed him as a prime minister's aide and placed him under Hosono. One of the problems they faced was contaminated water. On April 2 it became clear that water contaminated with radioactive substances was flowing from the Fukushima nuclear power plant into the Pacific Ocean, and work to stop this was undertaken.

One major concern at that time was the contamination of the groundwater. When the Fukushima Daiichi Nuclear Power Plant was originally constructed, a thirty-five-meter high bluff had been excavated to a height of ten meters. For this reason, a substantial volume of groundwater was to be found flowing beneath the site. In order to prevent the contaminated water from mixing with this groundwater, the insertion of steel plates extending down thirty-seven meters to bedrock was considered. I ordered that this be actively pursued, and it was included on the agenda we announced in April. But in keeping with fears that the construction costs would be too great, plans were scaled back, and after I retired from my position as prime minister it came to pass that an impermeable wall was placed sporadically along the coastward side of the site. As a result, the contaminated water flowing out of the structures housing the nuclear reactors continues to mix with the groundwater to this day.

Changing Direction

In addition to restoration work after the earthquake disaster and responding to the nuclear accident, I began to work on changes in our energy strategy, nuclear power included. In that context I would like to explain the circumstances of my gradual move away from the use of nuclear power.

My experience of the nuclear accident that began to unfold on March 11 changed my thinking about nuclear power. I came to understand that a nuclear accident carried with it a risk so large that it could lead to the collapse of a country. I became convinced that what we had been calling "safe nuclear power" could only be found through independence from nuclear power.

When I was first elected to office in 1980, the Socialist Democratic Federation of which I was a member defined nuclear power as a transitional energy, and it was with that point of view that I toured plants and asked questions at meetings of the Diet. Just the same, I did not believe we were in a position to extricate ourselves from a reliance on nuclear power, and prior to March 11, I thought we should make use of nuclear power plants if we had confirmed their safety. But after the accident on March 11, my way of thinking changed.

Let's say there is a chance of one accident every one hundred years. If we are talking about the odds that a car with several occupants will malfunction, one would say the risk is worth taking. But if there was a chance that an accident could put the whole planet in danger, regardless of whether an accident would occur once in one hundred or even one thousand years, no one would take that risk. That was the size of the risk we came face to face with in Fukushima. The only places on Earth that have earthquakes, tsunamis, and nuclear power plants are the West Coast of the United States and the Japanese islands. To make things worse, because Japan is not large, a nuclear accident could cause the entire country to stop functioning.

If we merely maintained our traditional approach to safety, the risks were too great to bear. The customary five layers of protection in a nuclear power plant could be increased to seven, and the seawall could be built still higher to protect against a tsunami, but ultimately with human error there would still be a chance that an accident might occur. An act of terrorism was another possibility. The international community has failed to resolve the threat of terror. People used to say that a nuclear power plant was safe as long as it was not struck directly by a missile. And yet the accident at Fukushima had taught the world's terrorists that a mere loss of electricity could cause a nuclear power plant to fall into an extreme state. Several dozen terrorists could invade a plant, cut the cables, and this alone would place all of Japan in a crisis.

When I considered such scenarios, my way of thinking changed. I came to believe that we must decrease our dependence on nuclear power and strive for a society that has no need for it. That is the safest way. This is how my thinking changed.

At the end of March, I gradually began to make public my move away from nuclear power. It was not covered in the press on a large scale, but meetings with the leaders of the Social Democratic Party and the Japanese Communist Party were the first steps.

Revisiting Our Energy Policy

At a meeting on March 30 with Mizuho Fukushima, leader of the Social Democratic Party, I suggested the need to reconsider the role of NISA. I also said, "Because there is a low percentage of renewable energy being used here in Japan, we must come up with a mechanism that encourages its increase." And I recall our discussing the fact that immediately prior to our meeting, in local elections in Germany, Alliance '90/The Greens had made great advances.

Then on March 31 I met with the Japanese Community Party's chairman Kazuo Shii and stated my opinion that all six reactors at the Fukushima Daiichi Nuclear Power Plant should be decommissioned. I also suggested that the Basic Energy Plan approved by the cabinet in June of the previous year [2010] be brought back to the table and reviewed. The Basic Energy Plan in question positioned nuclear power as the main source of energy and called for the construction of at least fourteen additional reactors by 2030. At this point I had decided we needed to decrease the number of reactors by fourteen.

Chairman Shii had come to request the abandonment of the energy plan, and I made this statement in that context. However, it is not as if I were deciding to revisit the energy plan because the Japanese Communist Party had asked me to. I had already come to the conclusion that the energy plan was unreasonable.

That same day I met with France's President Sarkozy, who had just arrived in Japan. At a joint press conference I said, "After a thorough investigation of the accident, there is a need to discuss our policy regarding nuclear and other energy." This bureaucratic language may be difficult for the general public to understand, but I was suggesting "a reconsideration of nuclear policy." It was essentially a declaration of war on the bureaucrats who were promoting nuclear power.

On April 18, at a meeting of the Standing Committee on Budget in the House of Councillors I was asked about our future nuclear energy policy. I responded, "Without a careful consideration of safety, we will not proceed with the plans we have had to date." Regarding the construction of additional reactors, I added, "Just because we decided on something doesn't mean we are committed to it." Finally, on the subject of the nuclear fuel cycle, I made my doubts clear when I said, "We must also investigate the storage of spent fuel in nuclear power plants given that the systems for its storage are not always secure."

I went still further on April 25 when, at a meeting of the House of Councillors' Audit Committee, I responded to a question by the Japanese Communist Party, saying, "In our thorough review of the basic energy policies previously decided on, I think we should consider going back to the drawing board."

Reparations

At a meeting of the Budget Committee of the House of Representatives on April 29, with regard to the matter of compensation, I suggested, "As the plant's operator, TEPCO should take primary responsibility." I said this in response to the suggestion that TEPCO should be exempt from the payment of reparations. According to article 3 of the Atomic Energy Damage Compensation Law, when nuclear damages are inflicted due to the operation of a nuclear reactor, the operator shall be responsible for compensation for damages, "but this will not apply when said damages result from an extraordinary natural disaster or a social upheaval."

I said that if we accepted this provision and concluded that TEPCO was exempt from responsibility, "if we determine that TEPCO is not responsible for reparations and the government will bear full responsibility for them, I don't think we are getting it right." I added that, after acknowledging TEPCO's primary responsibility, from a political and administrative perspective, I felt that the government should take responsibility for assuring that appropriate payments were made.

For the powers that be who thought TEPCO should be exempt from responsibility, my response must have been vexing.

Shutting Down Hamaoka

On May 6 I held a press conference and announced that I would be asking for the shutdown of Chubu Electric's Hamaoka Nuclear Power Plant. There has been much discussion and some speculation regarding this matter, so I would like to make a record here of my own perception of what happened.

On the previous day, on May 5, METI's Minister Kaieda visited Hamaoka. I had not directed him to do so. On the sixth, Minister Kaieda came to me and reported that he had inspected the Hamaoka Plant and thought it should be shut down. He had taken METI officials with him, so this could be understood as a sentiment that was shared within the ministry.

I had been thinking since late March that we needed to find a way to somehow shut down the Hamaoka Nuclear Power Plant. For some time it had been pointed out that the plant was in danger of a major accident resulting from an earthquake and tsunami [given its location near the junction of two tectonic plates], and members of the nuclear-free movement were quite outspoken about the need to halt its operation. The Ministry of Education, Culture, Sports, Science, and Technology's earthquake research group had also identified the risk of a major earthquake. Here I was thinking about how to stop its operation, and METI's Minister Kaieda came along saying he wanted to shut it down. Minister Kaieda said, "I knew how you felt about it, Mr. Kan," and I thought, "Is that so?"

Even in the face of an accident on the scale of Fukushima, METI had not moved away from the promotion of nuclear power. Given their pronuclear stance, I was surprised that the administrators at METI had agreed to the plan. But the administrative staff at METI appear to have drawn up a certain scenario. After the nuclear accident, they had been having difficulty restarting the nuclear power plants around the country that had been shut down for routine periodic inspections. Apparently, their strategy was to say, "We'll shut down Hamaoka because it's dangerous, but the other plants are safe, so we will restart them." I don't know the extent to which Minister Kaieda was aware of this scenario, but I can say that I knew nothing about it.

At around 1 p.m. on the sixth, Minister Kaieda called on me. He wanted to hold a press conference as soon as possible, but I asked him to hold off for the time being and we agreed to talk again that night. When we did talk, we decided that because the matter was of great importance I should hold a press conference. The press conference brief provided by METI clearly suggested that "Hamaoka is dangerous, so it should be shut down, but the other plants are safe. Those in use should continue to operate and those being inspected should be restarted." At the press conference, I made the following statement, making no reference to other nuclear power plants:

> I have an important announcement to make to the people of Japan. Today, in my capacity as prime minister, I requested through Banri Kaieda, the minister of METI, that the Chubu Electric Power Company suspend the operation of all nuclear reactors at the Hamaoka Nuclear Power Plant. I made this decision, first and foremost, in consideration of the safety and well-being of the general public. I came to this conclusion after contemplating what would happen if a major accident were to occur at the Hamaoka Nuclear Power Plant, and the enormous impact this would have on Japanese society as a whole.
>
> According to an assessment by the Headquarters for Earthquake Research Promotion of the Ministry of Education, Culture, Sports, Science, and Technology, there is an 87 percent chance of an earthquake of a magnitude of approximately 8.0 occurring in the Tokai region in the next thirty years. This is an extremely high probability. When one considers the special circumstances in which the Hamaoka Nuclear Power Plant finds itself, there is a need to implement sound mid- to long-term measures, such as the building of seawalls that will allow us to sufficiently withstand the earthquake and tsunami that are being predicted. In order to ensure the safety and well-being of the people, I have determined that the operation of all the Hamaoka reactors should be suspended until such measures have been taken. This should not only apply to Unit 3, which is currently stopped for a periodic inspection, but to all the reactors, including those now in operation.
>
> For a long time now the dangers associated with Hamaoka Nuclear Power Plant's location above an active fault have been known. After coming face to face with the recent earthquake and the resulting nuclear accident, I was compelled to listen to a variety of

opinions regarding the safety of the Hamaoka plant and to deliberate on this matter with Minister Kaieda of METI. This deliberation resulted in my decision today in my capacity as prime minister.

When the operation of the Hamaoka Nuclear Power Plant is suspended, the government will make every effort to ensure that this does not significantly disrupt Chubu Electric's internal power supply. I am confident that the risk of a power shortage can be overcome through creative efforts to further conserve power and energy on the part of those living near the plant and throughout Japan. I sincerely request the understanding and cooperation of the entire nation.

Because I handled the press conference in this way, the debate regarding the restart of nuclear power plants moved in a direction that was different from METI's original scenario. After I had turned METI's intentions on their head at Hamaoka, they did not consult with me when the matter of Kyushu Electric's Genkai Nuclear Power Plant came up. Rather, they prepared their own case in advance in an effort to make its restart a foregone conclusion.

This would place a strain on my relations with Minister Kaieda.

Energy Policy Shift

The cabinet did not have the authority to order Chubu Electric to halt the operation of a nuclear power plant. For this reason I took the approach of "calling for a shutdown," and I did not think that as a licensed enterprise the electric company would reject my request. Indeed, Chubu Electric decided to shut down the Hamaoka Nuclear Power Plant.

At a press conference on May 10, I announced that the government was preparing the establishment of a nuclear accident investigation committee. I suggested that the fundamental thinking behind this committee was transparency, comprehensiveness, and independence from the traditional administration of nuclear power. The committee would not only probe into technical matters but look at institutional and organizational problems as well. The establishment of this committee was approved by the cabinet on May 24.

At the same press conference I also spoke with regard to our future energy policy. "With nuclear power, it is more important than anything that we are able to assure safety. Where electricity is concerned, nuclear power and fossil fuels have functioned as two large pillars, but in light of the Fukushima accident and global warming, we must add renewable, natural energies such as solar, wind, and biomass (biological resources) as energy mainstays, and make the development of an energy-saving society another pillar of our energy policy as well."

I addressed the shifting of our energy policy in my response to a question from a reporter from Nishinippon Shimbun [a newspaper based in Kyushu] saying, "In the current Basic Energy Plan, a goal has been set for nuclear energy to make up 50 percent and renewable energy to account for 20 percent of total energy generation by the year 2030. But I believe that this major accident compels us to go back to the drawing board." I was essentially using this press conference as a public forum at which to declare my intention to start over again with regard to the Basic Energy Plan.

It can be said that at this point I was not calling for the phasing out of nuclear energy, but at a practical level I was beginning to head in that direction. Insofar as I was calling for the scrapping of a plan that had nuclear energy providing 50 percent of our power by the year 2030, it can be said that I was looking for a reduction of some sort.

Yoshihiko Noda's cabinet, which followed my own, took over the development of a new energy plan, moving forward while also asking widely for public opinion. This press conference was where it all began.

Beginning with the call for the shutdown of the Hamaoka Plant on May 6 and the establishment of stricter conditions for the restart of nuclear power plants, when I started to take a more definite stand against the use of nuclear power, the "nuclear village" [a vast and powerful network of vested interests] began attacking me through various media and politicians.

Their first such attack was related to the application of seawater. In his May 20 e-mail magazine, Shinzo Abe wrote with regard to flooding Unit 1 with seawater, "The injection of seawater began at 7:04 p.m. on March 12, and when this was reported to the office of the prime minister, Prime Minister Kan was infuriated, saying, 'I've heard nothing of this!' A telephone call was made from the prime minister's office to TEPCO, and the injection of seawater was stopped at 7:25 p.m. (text omitted) Prime Minister Kan should apologize to the people for his mistaken judgment and his lies, and he should resign." In this way, Abe was demanding my resignation. On the following day, May 21, Yomiuri Shimbun and Sankei Shimbun had front-page headlines and articles introducing Abe's suggestion that a meltdown had occurred because I had called a halt to the injection of seawater. This was far from the truth. As I explained in chapter 1, I was not informed that the application of seawater had begun and gave no orders to stop its use. Furthermore, it has been confirmed in an internal investigation conducted by TEPCO that when Ichiro Takeguro, TEPCO's liaison to my office, called Yoshida, the plant manager, to request that the application of seawater be halted, Yoshida determined the need to continue the injection and ignored Takeguro's orders. It has also been verified that the meltdown of Unit 1 occurred around 7 p.m. on March 11, prior to the application of seawater. This is to say that the articles in Yomiuri and Sankei and Abe's e-mail magazine were incorrect in every respect.

Thereafter, at the Diet, representatives of the Liberal Democratic Party repeatedly and relentlessly asked similar questions suggesting that I take responsibility for the meltdown. Then, on June 2, less than three months after the national crisis of a nuclear accident had occurred, a cabinet no-confidence motion was submitted. This was the product of the nuclear village's desire to pull me out of office and the Liberal Democratic Party's eagerness to return to a position of power. I was reminded of the statement in Gorbachev's memoirs that "there were a few who tried to treat Chernobyl as a subject for political speculation." Fortunately, this no-confidence motion was rejected.

Promoting Renewables

In the latter half of May, efforts to drive me out of office increased, and there was a growing sense of my political jeopardy. I was scheduled to attend a G8 summit in Deauville, France, on May 25. At an event in Paris commemorating the fiftieth anniversary of the OECD I expressed Japan's goal of "renewable energy exceeding 20 percent of total power generation as early in the 2020s as possible."

In concrete terms, I announced our intention to reduce the cost of solar power generation to one-third of present-day costs by 2020 and one-sixth by the year 2030, and to place solar panels on the roofs of 10 million homes by then as well. In addition to solar, I also emphasized our promotion of the development of large-scale offshore wind power, next-generation biofuels, and geothermal power generation. Toward the end of the Deauville Summit, the

Japanese people were commended for their fortitude in the face of a major earthquake disaster, and the meeting ended in a generally positive mood. I returned to Japan on May 29.

As I mentioned above, the ultimate "drop Kan" move came with the submission on June 2 of a "Kan Cabinet No-Confidence Motion." When I made my antinuclear stance clear, Ichiro Ozawa, former leader of the Democratic Party, approached former prime minister Yoshiro Mori of the Liberal Democratic Party, saying that if Mori submitted a motion of no confidence, the members of Ozawa's group would support him. According to a July 7, 2012, interview with Mori in the Sankei Shimbun, Ozawa had made him an offer: "If the LDP submits a no-confidence motion, we'll join you. If you topple the Kan cabinet, we'll nominate Sadakazu Tanigaki as prime minister and form a grand alliance."

In order to avoid a no-confidence decision, at a meeting of representatives immediately prior to a plenary session of the House of Councillors on June 2, I said, "When we have accomplished certain goals with regard to the handling of the earthquake disaster and I have fulfilled my role, I want to pass my responsibilities on to the next generation." As a result, former prime minister and party representative Hatoyama and most of the Democratic Party representatives voted against the no-confidence motion and it was rejected by a wide margin. Mr. Ozawa was absent at the time of the vote.

A prime minister's term is not defined in the constitution or in the official cabinet law. When a cabinet's no-confidence motion carries, one has no choice but to dissolve the cabinet or for the cabinet to resign en masse. When the cabinet is dissolved or when one's term of office as a representative expires, at the first meeting of the Diet after a general election, the cabinet resigns en masse and a new prime minister is nominated. This is the only matter defined in the constitution. For this reason, one's term as prime minister and one's term as a representative are connected to a certain degree.

Unrelated to the number of years I personally wanted to remain in office, at a fundamental level I did not think it was in the national interest to change prime ministers after only a short tenure. In principle, if a change of regime was achieved through an election, I thought we should make a custom of the prime minister serving a four-year term. But I had promised that "when we have achieved certain goals, I will hand things over to someone who is younger," and in a situation where the breaking up of the Democratic Party had to be avoided, I determined that it was impossible to remain prime minister until the end of my term as an elected representative. It was for this reason that at a press conference later that same day, I said that I would resign "when we have achieved certain earthquake disaster recovery and reconstruction goals and the containment of the nuclear accident."

During my tenure as prime minister, I wanted to realize the passage of an important bill, a bill to promote renewable energy. This legislation would require utilities to purchase, at a fixed price, electricity generated through the use of renewable energy. This would spur on the diffusion of renewable energy and, as a result, help move us away from nuclear power generation. It just so happens that this bill had been approved by my cabinet on March 11, immediately prior to the earthquake, and that it had been submitted to the Diet.

Beginning in the fall of the previous year [2010] I had brought in a friend of thirty years, the journalist Kenichi Shimomura, to act as the vice minister for policy coordination, and I had asked him to handle public relations. At his suggestion a place was set aside on the home page of the Prime Minister's Office for me to write a blog. It was there that beginning on June 6, I wrote intermittently about energy issues. In my first entry I wrote the following:

My Experience with Wind Energy

The government has submitted to the current session of the Diet a bill that represents a significant step toward "a new era." It has been thirty years in the making. Late in 1980, when I was first elected to the Diet, I traveled to the United States to visit with a large number of citizens' groups. During my time there I went to the National Wind Test Center, which was testing dozens of wind-power generation devices outside Denver.

When I asked what they did with the power generated, I was told that it was sold to a power company through a backward feed over their transmission lines. If this were true, one could make effective use of privately generated electricity that remained unconsumed. On returning to Japan, I immediately set to work to see if we could do the same thing here, but I ran into a large wall—also known as the Electricity Business Act—which restricts the electricity purchased by power companies.

Domestically, the Science and Technology Agency had launched a test wind-generation project called the "Wind-Topia Plan," and I showed my support by bringing it up in the Diet. I also toured two large wind-power-generating facilities that TEPCO had set up on Miyake Island. The project was ultimately called off, however, when it was determined that it was not profitable.

More than thirty years have passed since I was first elected to office. During that time, wind and solar power have been treated as a nuisance by electric companies. Despite having excellent technologies, we have not developed them in earnest. As a result, we have fallen dramatically behind our European counterparts.

In the wake of the recent nuclear accident I want to go back to the drawing board with regard to the Basic Energy Plan and cultivate wind, solar, and other renewable energies as core energies of "a new era." A major step in that direction is a system whereby electricity generated from natural, renewable sources is purchased at a fixed price. If we are able to achieve this, we will succeed in breaking through the legal wall I ran into when I was a newly elected legislator.

We have come a long way, even reaching a cabinet decision to submit a bill to the Diet. That decision was made on March 11, but a major earthquake struck that same day. While this caused a slight delay, we have presented this bill to the current Diet session. If we are able to turn this bill into a law and promptly establish economically viable pricing, we can expect wind and solar power generation to expand at an explosive pace.

Ultimately, a bill to promote renewable energy was passed on August 26, 2011. It was the final achievement of my administration. It was broadcast on the news, so became quite well known, but I provoked the Diet by saying, "There are those in the Diet who do not want to see my face. If you don't want to look at me, please pass the renewable-energy bill at the earliest possible date. By so doing, our respective goals will be in sight."

My Smile Returns, I Am Told

When I halted the operation of the Hamaoka Nuclear Power Plant, there were those who interpreted this as a move away from the use of nuclear power and who came out to support me, but it was not until a concrete goal was attained in the form of the bill to promote renewable energy that activities to phase out nuclear power became a more definable movement.

On June 7, at the ninth meeting of the Council for the Realization of a New Growth Strategy, the discussion centered on innovative energy and environmental strategy. While it is certainly meaningful for those in the movement to call for the elimination nuclear power, the government must make this part of an overall energy strategy. Otherwise it is nothing more than pie in the sky. At the beginning of the meeting I said: "The expansion of our country's economy and the realization of a paradigm shift involving new energies rests on our ability to put ideas into practice. I want to make that happen." In order to phase out nuclear energy, we absolutely need something to replace it.

On Sunday, June 12, we held an open roundtable conference regarding renewable energy, the Prime Minister-Experts Open Forum on Natural Energy, in the prime minister's office compound. I was joined by many experts, and the roundtable was broadcast live on the Internet. Professor Hiroshi Tasaka of Tama University Graduate School, who had agreed to be a special adviser to the cabinet, led the discussion. It was attended by SoftBank Corp.'s president Masayoshi Son, former head coach of Japan's national soccer team Takeshi Okada, environmental journalist Junko Edahiro, AP Bank representative director Takeshi Kobayashi, and musician and environmental activist Ryuichi Sakamoto, who participated by means of a video link with New York City. It was a very meaningful meeting.

In an opening statement, I said:

> Traditionally, fossil fuels and nuclear power have been two major pillars of our national energy plan, but we need to add natural, renewable energy and energy conservation as well. The development of these new energies is extremely important to Japan's growth and, of course, to Japanese society. (text omitted) In keeping with my current position, with regard to the direction our government is going, I have suggested that we should achieve at least 20 percent renewable energy sometime early in the 2020s.

During the meeting I spoke of natural energy from two positions, weaving together statements made in my capacity as Japan's chief executive and comments as an individual. For this reason I was able to speak more naturally than usual, and I received a considerable number of favorable responses.

Since the earthquake disaster and nuclear accident there had been very few occasions to laugh, and when it appeared that we had extricated ourselves from the worst of the nuclear crisis, a severe political situation awaited me. So this open forum was the first time I had enjoyed myself in a long time. Those who attended had no relation to the political situation, and I was able to talk of science, a subject I have always been fond of. And when I discussed my own pet theory that "plants will, in fact, save the planet," there was a moment there when I enjoyed being teased by Kumi Fujisawa (cofounder of the think tank SophiaBank) who was emceeing the meeting.

In the course of the meeting I distinctly felt the existence of a large groundswell to promote the spread of renewable energy. For some time I had been hearing of various individual initiatives, but I was struck by the sense that these individual points had begun to spread out and form a plane. Through the experience of a nuclear accident, individual citizens had begun to think about what they should do.

Another open forum, entitled Open Dialogue with the Public on Natural Energy, was held the following week. This time I responded to questions that had been sent through Twitter on June 12, during the Prime Minister-Experts Open Forum on Natural Energy. I also exchanged messages via live video relay with audience participation groups that had gathered in various locations throughout the country. In my opening address I said, "Again today, in addition to taking responsibility for what I say as prime minister, I also want to convey my own personal thoughts and feelings."

Around this time we also established the Energy and Environment Council under the auspices of the National Policy Unit. Energy policy that would traditionally have been entrusted to METI alone could now be developed across all the ministries, the

Ministry for the Environment and the Ministry of Agriculture, Forestry, and Fisheries among them. The council's first meeting was held on June 22.

Such administrative reforms would come to have great importance in moving away from nuclear energy.

Reconstruction

A meeting of the Reconstruction Design Council in Response to the Great East Japan earthquake was held on June 25, and I was handed a proposal entitled "Toward Reconstruction: Hope beyond the Disaster" by Dr. Makoto Iokibe, chair of the council. The first meeting of the council had been held on April 14, and this was the twelfth meeting.

Taking the document in hand, I said, "I am confident that this is a useful and lasting proposal that addresses major economic, social, and community issues and the problem of the nuclear accident as well. From this point forward, I would like to make use of this proposal to the fullest possible extent in advancing reconstruction. While the Basic Act on Reconstruction has already been enacted and promulgated, at the beginning of next week I intend to create a Reconstruction Headquarters to formulate guidelines based on this proposal."

The Basic Act on Reconstruction was passed on June 20. In keeping with its enactment, there was a need to create a new minister, a minister for reconstruction, and I was finally able to add a cabinet member. I asked Ryu Matsumoto, who had, since the earthquake disaster, put his heart and soul into the recovery and reconstruction of the disaster-stricken areas in the capacity of minister of state for disaster management, to become the minister for reconstruction. Shortly thereafter, Minister Matsumoto would resign over comments he made on the occasion of a visit to a hard-hit area, but he had performed his duties well as minister of state for disaster management. Thereafter he was stationed at the Crisis Management Center in the basement of the prime minister's office building where he took command of the situation, often forgetting to eat or sleep. Minister Matsumoto had made many visits to the devastated areas and listened more than anyone else to the people he met there.

We need to continue our support of the devastated areas, Fukushima included.

Another Minister

On June 26, in addition to Minister of Reconstruction Matsumoto, I made Special Adviser Hosono the minister for the restoration from and prevention of nuclear accidents. The reason I ventured to make Special Adviser Hosono a minister at this time was because I wanted to lay the groundwork for a fundamental reevaluation of the administration of nuclear power. Minister Kaieda agreed that NISA should be separated from METI. To be absolutely sure that this would occur I wanted to have a minister who would be responsible for the handling of the nuclear accident. The person most suited to this position was Special Adviser Hosono, who had been continuously responsible for the handling of the nuclear accident since March as the secretariat of the Government-TEPCO Integrated Response Office.

Up to this point, the only related ministerial post was the minister of the pronuclear METI. Now I was able to appoint a minister with regulatory authority. While Kasumigaseki's bureaucrats [Kasumigaseki being the center of the Japanese bureaucracy] did not feel compelled to report to special advisers to the prime minister, they were instilled with a sense of responsibility to report to ministers. With the appointment of Special Adviser Hosono as a minister, a check-and-balance dynamic was achieved within the cabinet, and within the government. It was my understanding that from the moment I placed Minister Hosono in this pivotal position for the reform of nuclear power, we had entered a second stage, in which nuclear power's close-knit structure could be reevaluated.

At the press conference at which I announced this appointment I also made public for the first time the three conditions for my resignation: the achievement of a second supplementary budget, the passage of a renewable-energy bill, and the passage of a bill for special provisions concerning the issuance of government bonds.

Restarting the Genkai Plant

As I described above, after the shutdown of the Hamaoka Nuclear Power Plant had been achieved, and without any explanation to me, METI began preparing for the restart of the Genkai Nuclear Power Plant. Apparently they thought it would be easy to gain the approval of the local government in Saga Prefecture, where the Genkai Nuclear Power Plant is located.

After Minister Kaieda visited Saga Prefecture, I learned—through the media—that Saga's governor Yasushi Furukawa "wants to know the prime minister's opinion." I believed that any decision should be based on a thorough review of the plant's safety. With this in mind, I queried Minister Kaieda, "Have you asked the Nuclear Safety Commission [NSC] what they think and adequately confirmed that the plant is safe?" Unable to answer, Minister Kaieda turned to a nearby bureaucrat who said, "According to existing laws, it is possible to proceed with the restarting of a plant based solely on the judgment of NISA. We have not asked the opinion of the NSC." To this, I responded, "Even if pre-March 11 laws have it so, we cannot expect to gain the understanding of the public based only on the judgment of an organization that was unable to prevent the accident at the Fukushima nuclear power plant." For this reason, I ordered the engagement of the NSC and the introduction of stress tests.

On June 21, at the International Atomic Energy Agency's Ministerial Conference on Nuclear Safety, Director-General Amano proposed a "review of the safety of all nuclear power plants," and this was endorsed by all member states. This meant the application of "stress tests" that anticipated the occurrence of a large natural disaster and other extreme scenarios. A provisional appraisal of the accident at the Fukushima Daiichi Nuclear Power Plant was also presented at this conference, which Minister Kaieda also attended.

With the IAEA conference as a backdrop, and with the goal of developing concrete conditions for the restarting of nuclear power plants, I asked Minister Kaieda, Minister Hosono, and Chief Cabinet Secretary Edano to draw up provisional rules that the public would find satisfactory and that could be implemented until fully developed legal reforms were made. They decided that, in addition to stress tests, the key when determining whether or not to restart a nuclear power plant was the NSC's participation, the consent of the local government, and ultimately the approval of four individuals: the minister of METI, the minister for the restoration from and prevention of nuclear accidents, the chief cabinet secretary, and the prime minister.

In early July, it was uncovered that the governor of Saga and Kyushu Electric may have colluded in encouraging employees of the electric and other related companies to attend a public meeting and speak favorably of the restarting of reactor units 2 and 3 of the Genkai Nuclear Power Plant. When this story came to light, the restarting of the Genkai plant became far more difficult.

Stress Tests

On July 12, 2011, I made the following entry with regard to stress tests in my blog on the prime minister's official homepage:

A cabinet consensus opinion was compiled yesterday regarding the recent introduction of stress tests for Japan's nuclear reactors. I had requested the "formulation of rules that would be acceptable to the public," and I think we have succeeded in putting together a document that makes progress in this regard. This was not a conclusion reached lightly. It was arrived at through a careful consideration of public safety and peace of mind.

The Nuclear and Industrial Safety Agency [NISA] is situated within METI, so we must resolve this contradiction of having the same entity responsible for "promoting" and "monitoring" nuclear power as soon as possible. I would like to note that we have already declared this in a report submitted to the International Atomic Energy Agency, so this is not something that is being brought up suddenly now for the first time.

In this context, it goes without saying that decisions regarding the restarting of nuclear reactors cannot be left to NISA alone in its current configuration. Hence our recent policy decision to involve an independent entity, the NSC, while we search for the ideal regulatory structure. Meanwhile, the government must also ensure another form of peace of mind by shouldering responsibility for the supply of electrical power. With this in mind, I have asked policy makers to consider strategies for the utilization of corporate in-house power generation and innovative energy conservation to ensure the supply of electricity.

We must wipe the slate clean when considering an energy plan. We must introduce renewable energies over the middle and long term, promote energy conservation, and break free of our dependence on nuclear power. To what extent can we give form to this resolve in our daily lives? Today I will continue to give my all!

With stricter conditions for the authorization of the restart of the nuclear power plants that had been stopped for periodic and other inspections, the twenty-seven nuclear reactors that were being operated in Japan at the time of the accident did not receive authorization for reactivation. By May 2012 all the reactors were dormant. Later that same year two reactors in Fukui were reactivated, and they operated until September 2013, when they were shut down once again for periodic inspections. In keeping with this, all of Japan's nuclear reactors have been shut down since November 2013.[1] Thereafter, through the conservation of power and an increase in the generation of power through nonnuclear means, we have been able to meet our electricity needs, thereby proving that we could go about our lives and enjoy economic activity without any great confusion, even in the absence of nuclear power.

Nuclear Power–Free Declaration

In a press conference on July 13, I declared my resolve to "strive for a society that is not dependent on nuclear power." I have excerpted the applicable portions below.

I would like to clarify my thoughts related to nuclear power and energy policy. Prior to my experience of the nuclear accident on March 11, my policy on nuclear power was that it should be utilized, while ensuring its safety, and I made statements to that effect. However, in the course of experiencing this major nuclear accident, I came to understand the scale of the risks involved. Residents living within a ten-kilometer radius and then a twenty-kilometer radius had to be evacuated. But in a worst-case scenario, evacuations from an even wider area might have been necessary. And with regard to the containment of the accident, while it might be possible to advance certain areas to step 1 [wherein radiation levels are in steady decline] or step 2 [wherein the release of radioactive materials is under control and radiation levels are being significantly held down], it may take five, ten, or even more years for a reactor core to be decommissioned.

When I considered the scale of the risks arising from a nuclear accident, I realized it would no longer be possible to conduct policy on the basis of ensuring safety alone, which was the conventional wisdom prior to the accident. I became painfully aware that this was the kind of technology we were dealing with.

It is in this context that I have come to the conclusion that, with regard to Japan's future energy policy, we should aim to achieve a society that is not dependent on nuclear power. I have come to think that we should reduce our dependence on nuclear power in a planned and gradual manner and strive for a society that thrives without it. I have come to believe that this is the direction our country should pursue.

On the other hand, the government is also responsible for the supply of power required by people going about their lives and by industry as well. With the understanding and cooperation of the members of the public and corporations involved, I believe that through power saving during peak demand times over the summer months and through the utilization of privately owned power generation, we can respond in a manner this situation requires of us. In this regard, I have already given instructions to the responsible ministers to draft a plan for the supply of power.

The measures for which I have issued instructions to date, including the request to suspend the operation of the Hamaoka Nuclear Power Plant and the introduction of stress tests, have been intended to ensure public safety and peace of mind. These instructions have been given based on the fundamental and unwavering perception of nuclear power I have just described. In particular, the problem of having NISA, which is responsible for monitoring safety, positioned under METI, which currently supports the use of nuclear power, is one that has already been flagged in a report submitted to the International Atomic Energy Agency (IAEA) concerning the need to separate these two bodies. This is a problem recognized by the government and by the minister of METI. For not addressing this matter sooner, I would like to reiterate my apologies to those whom I have inconvenienced.

I hereby conclude a description of my thoughts with regard to nuclear power plants and nuclear power. From here forward, in keeping therewith, I will continue to make every effort to engage in a fundamental reform of the administration of nuclear power, and work actively to secure new renewable energy sources and to promote energy conservation.

I was asked if the entire government was for the elimination of nuclear power, and I responded that officially these statements reflected my personal opinion. Indeed, it was not a cabinet decision, and no coordination of the ministries had occurred. Nonetheless, I thought it was important and only natural for me, in my position at the top, to state my personal thoughts and to clarify the direction I thought we should be headed in. And I would work to see that the elimination of nuclear power became government policy.

On July 29, two weeks after my "antinuclear" press conference, at an energy and environment meeting attended by the entire cabinet, we decided to "reduce our dependence on nuclear power." Further, in creating a strategy for the realization of this aim, we decided that in addition to input from the government and experts, we would also be required to make use of ideas coming from the Japanese people.

At the conclusion of the meeting, I said the following:

Today, the government has taken up an innovative energy and environmental strategy. With this interim arrangement as a foundation, and after another year or more of debate, I hope the cabinet and the government will make every effort to ultimately see this through to its completion. This is my sincere wish.

What we decided at the meeting that day was continued by the Noda administration, and debated widely by the people. A little more than a year later, in September 2012, it led to our commitment to the accomplishment of a total elimination of nuclear power by the 2030s.

Consumption Tax and Social Security

Ever since I assumed the office of prime minister, I wanted to do whatever I could to achieve the comprehensive reform of social security and consumption tax. With the aging of Japanese society, there has been an annual increase of 1 trillion yen [US$9.8 billion at 102 yen/$1] in disbursements by the national treasury for medical care, pensions, nursing, and other social-welfare services for the elderly. In the past ten years all additional disbursements have been paid for with government bonds, or, in other words, with borrowed money.

The Liberal Democrats, who had long been in power, would certainly have known this. But even during Junichiro Koizumi's highly popular administration from 2001 to 2006, this problem was put off. When I was finance minister during the Hatoyama administration—from 2009 to 2010—I experienced the Greek debt crisis. And while most of Japan's government bonds are absorbed domestically, that is no cause for peace of mind. If the market were to perceive Japanese bonds as a risk, interest rates might suddenly rise.

It was with this sense of impending danger that immediately after assuming the office of prime minister and while facing an election for the House of Councillors, I expressed my interest in considering an increase in the consumption tax. I suggested that, in terms of an actual percentage, I wanted to use the LDP's 10 percent rate as a reference. The House of Councillors election did not go well, and I feel responsible for many of my friends losing their seats. I also feel responsible for the fact that this resulted in a divided Diet in which the two houses were controlled by different parties, making the management of Diet affairs all the more difficult.

But when it came to the comprehensive reform of social security and consumption tax, I felt there should be no distinction between ruling and opposition parties. I wanted to address this matter without political tensions. When he was still a member of the Liberal Democratic Party, Representative Kaoru Yosano had worked to increase the consumption tax and coordinated other fiscal reforms as the chairman of a financial reform study group. Thereafter, he had served as a joint representative of the Sunrise Party of Japan, although more recently he was not affiliated with any party. In January of 2011, in a reshuffling of the cabinet, I asked Mr. Yosano to join the cabinet as a minister to handle the comprehensive reform of social security and consumption tax.

In this way, without a party affiliation and acting as a minister of the Democratic Party and the People's New Party coalition government, Kaoru Yosano worked furiously for the comprehensive reform of social security and the consumption tax. And he continued to dedicate all his energy to this cause, while I devoted large amounts of my time to addressing the aftermath of the earthquake disaster. Then, on June 30, the Government and Ruling Parties Social Security Reform Study Headquarters agreed on a final draft of the comprehensive reform of social security and consumption tax, and the guiding principles for a social security and tax identification number.

Preparing to Step Down

In Japan, August is a time to reflect on the terrible power of the atom. I attended a peace memorial ceremony in Hiroshima on the sixth, and another in Nagasaki on the ninth. At the ceremony in Hiroshima, I said the following (and something similar in Nagasaki as well) about nuclear power and energy:

> We are starting from scratch in an effort to revise our energy policy. I deeply regret having believed in the nuclear power "safety myth." I will carry out a thorough investigation of the causes of the Fukushima accident and implement fundamental measures to ensure greater safety. At the same time, Japan will reduce its level of reliance on nuclear power generation with the aim of becoming a society that is not dependent on it.
>
> Interpreting this accident as a new lesson for all of humanity, I believe it is our responsibility to communicate what we have learned to the people of the world and to future generations.

On August 15, the cabinet decided that the nuclear safety regulation branch of NISA would be separated from METI. A nuclear safety and security agency [later named the Nuclear Regulation Authority] would be established as an external bureau under the jurisdiction of the Ministry of the Environment; this agency would handle all nuclear safety regulatory business.

On August 26, the bill for special provisions concerning the issuance of government bonds and the bill for the promotion of renewable energy passed. Because the second supplementary budget had already been approved, all three items I had attached importance to had been approved, and I announced that I would resign from my position as representative of the Democratic Party.

My Final Address

While it is common for the texts of press conferences to be prepared by government officials, for the most part mine were not. In particular, my final address, on August 26, in which I resigned from my position as prime minister, incorporated my own sentiments. It was a product of deliberation with the staff appointed to the prime minister's office who had supported me during my term. I would like you to read it.

> Immediately after I took office, the Democratic Party of Japan lost control of the House of Councillors, creating a divided Diet. Within the Democratic Party as well, although I was reelected last September and have enjoyed the support of a large number of people inside and outside the party, the situation has been difficult. Nevertheless, I have promoted policies that truly benefit the people of Japan, and my cabinet has done everything it could to address all manner of domestic and foreign issues over the past fifteen months.
>
> I honestly believe, as I stand ready to leave this post, that I did what was required of me in very difficult circumstances. The cabinet has made definite progress, working for recovery and reconstruction after the Great East Japan earthquake, containing the nuclear accident, and working on the comprehensive reform of our social security and consumption tax. I may be too optimistic, but when I think of what my cabinet accomplished under such harsh conditions, I feel a certain sense of achievement.
>
> I was not born into a family of politicians, and I got my start as a participant in a citizens' movement. I was only able to take on the heavy responsibilities of this office and accomplish the things I wanted to accomplish thanks to the support I received from the

public, and in particular those among the local electorate who backed me without any thought of personal gain. I am truly grateful to all of you.

When I assumed the office of prime minister, I said that I wanted to create a society with as little unhappiness as possible. Regardless of the nation or the era, I firmly believe that the principal aim of government should be the reduction of unhappiness among the people. That is why, where the economy is concerned, I put so much energy into the creation of jobs. The loss of one's job is not just a financial hardship. It is the loss of a place where one belongs, a place where one can play a role. It is a major cause of unhappiness. When I pursued the New Growth Strategy, I placed great emphasis on the creation of opportunities for employment. I also set up a number of task forces to address a wide range of issues that had been previously overlooked. Among these, I sought to recover the remains of the war dead from Iwo Jima, to fight incurable diseases and viruses, and to prevent suicide and social isolation.

After experiencing the Great East Japan earthquake on March 11 and the nuclear accident that followed, I became all the more convinced of the need to achieve a society with as little unhappiness as possible. Because Japan is located on one of the most earthquake-prone archipelagos in the world and home to a large number of nuclear power plants, this experience has taught us that an accident can threaten the future of our country and its people.

As the prime minister, I felt painfully powerless and unprepared when I was unable to prevent the Fukushima nuclear accident from occurring and so many people from suffering. I have heard the voices of the Japanese people, and in particular the profound concerns of families with small children, and I will do my utmost to continue to address this problem until my very last day as prime minister.

Thinking back, for the first week after the earthquake occurred I remained in my office day and night, trying to keep the situation under control. A number of nuclear reactors were damaged and hydrogen explosions occurred one after another. Working to prevent the nuclear damage from spreading, I spent those days in great fear, for once a nuclear accident spreads, there is no avoiding the evacuation of a wide area for a long time.

So how should we address a risk that threatens the very existence of our country? The answer I found was to strive for a society that is not dependent on nuclear power. That is the conclusion I reached.

I was reminded once again that nuclear accidents must be viewed in the context of the nuclear village, which influences both the way we inspect and regulate nuclear power and the relationship between government and industry, and ultimately extends into issues of culture. It was for this reason that I worked, not only to contain the nuclear accident, but to thoroughly reevaluate and reform energy policy and the administration of nuclear power.

I have initiated a public debate on everything from the safety and cost of nuclear power to the nuclear fuel cycle, leaving nothing sacred, nothing untouched. Even after I step down, it is my responsibility, as a politician who was prime minister during a major earthquake disaster and nuclear accident, to continue to do everything in my power to listen to the victims of this disaster, to work on measures for the handling of radiation pollution, to fundamentally reform the administration of nuclear power, and to realize a society free from any dependence on nuclear power.

Enduring great hardships and striving to overcome an unprecedented earthquake disaster and nuclear accident, the Japanese people have joined together as one. Witnessing the work of the police officers, firefighters, Japan Coast Guard personnel, Self-Defense Forces personnel, and the on-site workers who, since immediately after the earthquake disaster, have been risking their lives in the rescue and relief effort and in responding to the nuclear accident, I am filled with tremendous pride.

In particular, as commander in chief, I have been deeply moved by the activities of the Self-Defense Forces as they have shown everyone their true meaning as an organization that exists to serve this country and its people.

And I want to take this opportunity to express my deep respect and gratitude to the survivors of the disaster who are trying to make it through to tomorrow, to the local governments in the disaster-affected areas who are trying to support them, and to the many people of this nation who are providing them with such warm support.

We, the Japanese people, received the world's praise for our spirit of sharing and compromise after the earthquake disaster. And this was followed by the material and spiritual support of many of the world's countries. We must rebuild and become a country that is capable of repaying these kindnesses. I feel this now more than ever.

In particular, the US government's Operation Tomodachi was tangible proof of the true importance of the Japan-US alliance. Viewed from a security perspective, the world continues to be an unstable place. Continuing our foreign policy with the Japan-US alliance as its cornerstone, we must maintain a strong commitment to protecting the security of Japan and the world.

At the Japan-China-Republic of Korea Trilateral Summit held in Japan in May, both visiting leaders took a trip to the disaster area. I believe we were able to share an understanding of the importance of supporting one another during disasters and in times of need.

Many governments around the world are currently facing very difficult fiscal situations. In the days leading up to the House of Councillors' election, shortly after I became prime minister, I called for the initiation of talks about social security and the use of consumption tax as a means to fund rising social security costs. This matter was debated thereafter, and this June we completed a concrete plan for the comprehensive reform of social security and consumption tax.

Securing the sustainability of the social-security and consumption-tax systems is an issue that no administration can avoid, and it is fundamental to the realization of a society with the least unhappiness. When we look at the examples other countries have set for us, it is obvious that we cannot put this matter off any longer. This is a difficult issue, but I want the understanding of the people and the cooperation of both the ruling and opposition parties in making this happen. I entreat you.

I leave the question of how I will be judged for the work I have done during my time as prime minister to future generations. All that has ever mattered to me has been to move forward with regard to the issues that lie before me, in the context of the conditions that I find myself in. That is all that has mattered to me.

I deeply regret that I was not able to express my thoughts better to the public or to push matters forward more smoothly within the constraints of a divided Diet. But even in this context, I purposefully took on difficult and controversial issues. My only explanation for this is that as a member of the baby-boom generation, I have been driven by the strong conviction that we must not foist our problems on future generations.

Fiscally unsustainable governance, the social security system, the creation of an agricultural industry that young people can participate in, energy supply and demand after the Great East Japan earthquake—I believe these are all problems that my generation has a responsibility to find appropriate policies for before we pass the baton to younger generations. If nothing else, I sincerely hope that those who take on this responsibility after me will share in this conviction. That said, may this serve as my resignation address.

3

The Road to a Nuclear-Free Japan

As I said in my final address, my regrets at the time of my resignation were with regard to the survivors of the earthquake and tsunami and the victims of the nuclear accident. Now, long after the earthquake, many continue to live in painful circumstances. We must continue to give them comprehensive, long-term support. And those who were forced to evacuate and are unable to return to homes that remain entirely intact but are located near the Fukushima nuclear power plant bear a tremendous psychological burden. I believe we need to do everything we can to support the rebuilding of their lives because their suffering continues.

What then should be done about nuclear power? How should we proceed with our energy policy? Major issues remained undecided. In order to move away from the use of nuclear energy, there is a need to increase the use of alternative and renewable energies.

Visiting Renewable Energy Sites

After resigning, I traveled to Germany, which had turned the Fukushima nuclear accident into a new opportunity to phase out nuclear power; to Spain, which is expanding the use of renewable energy by separating electrical power production from its distribution and transmission; to Denmark, with its advanced systems for district heating through the supply of thermal energy; and to Sacramento, California, which had accomplished a regional departure from the use of nuclear power.

In 2000, led by a Social Democratic Party and Green Party coalition government (the Red-Green alliance), Germany had already decided to end its reliance on nuclear power by 2022. Thereafter, under Chancellor Merkel's conservative government, the deadline for an end to nuclear power had been extended to 2036. Once a physicist, Merkel was deeply concerned, however, that if a major nuclear accident could occur in as technologically advanced a country as Japan, it could also happen in Germany. Within several months after the Fukushima nuclear accident she decided to reset the deadline to 2022. This decision was made after the first lengthy national debate of this issue since the nuclear accident at Chernobyl in 1986. The people I met with, businesspeople and laborers alike, had accepted this decision, and I was under the impression that a national consensus had been reached.

In Spain, the percentage of energy generated through wind and solar power is high. They are separating electrical power production from its distribution and transmission, with one company handling generation and another responsible for transmission. Modulations in the renewable energy generated are being managed by a single, national control center.

In Denmark, at the time of the oil shock, people protested against nuclear power plants the government had planned to build. After a national debate the choice was made to be nuclear-free. Renewable energy is widely used, with an emphasis on wind power, and Vestas, one of the world's largest manufacturers of wind turbines, is native to Denmark.

In Sacramento, California, local residents voted to halt operation of the Rancho Seco Nuclear Generating Station in June 1989. Thereafter, the Sacramento Municipal Utility District has moved to conserve energy and to pursue other green efforts that have improved the financial condition of what was once a fiscally troubled operation. I learned a lot from their revolutionary consumer-as-participant approach, making use of demand response and other innovations.

I also toured many sites in Japan, visiting companies working with renewable energy and energy conservation, and visiting wind, solar, and biomass generation facilities. Along the way, I listened to what experts in these areas had to say.

In this way, in the year immediately following my resignation, I intensively researched the potential for renewable energy and energy conservation. As a result I am confident that in Japan we can adequately supply the electricity we need without making use of nuclear power.

The True Cost of Nuclear Power

While more and more people are calling for an end to nuclear power, many, especially in the business community, adamantly profess its necessity. It was reported that at a summit of business leaders someone had suggested that "a world without nuclear power plants is unthinkable." I am curious to know what they really mean by this. Do they believe the myth that nuclear power can be safe and that a major nuclear accident is out of the question? I am dumbfounded by arguments that pretend the Fukushima nuclear accident never occurred.

Some in business here in Japan say, "If our nuclear power plants aren't in operation, Japan's economy will suffer." But I want to ask them if they have considered just how great the damage to Japan's economy would have been if, as a result of the nuclear accident in Fukushima, we'd had to evacuate the 30 million people living in the Tokyo metropolitan area. Doubtless Japan would have suffered a state of total confusion, a fiscal, social, and international crisis that would have threatened our very existence. We were spared this scenario by a hair, a very thin line. And we cannot expect an accident to ever unfold in the same way again.

We, the Japanese people, should share an understanding that the nuclear accident we experienced at Fukushima was a crisis that threatened our existence as a nation. That is the place we should start from. Arguments that forget or ignore this are out of touch with reality.

The accident at the Fukushima nuclear power plant made it clear that nuclear power is not an enterprise for which a single private company is capable of taking full responsibility. This is to say, the very foundation of the "nuclear power is cheap" argument has collapsed.

First of all, the cost of constructing nuclear power plants has risen worldwide as people increasingly call for stricter safety standards. And what will the cost of damages for the Fukushima accident be? Many people lost their homes and their jobs. Many were forced to live away from their families. Tens of thousands of lives were destroyed. While it is impossible to put a monetary value on those damages, according to calculations by the Cost Verification Committee at the National Policy Unit it approaches 6 trillion yen [US$58.8 billion at 102 yen/$1]. This includes 1.2 trillion yen for TEPCO's decommissioning of the reactors, 2.6 trillion yen for the tentative payment of compensation for damages (with a payment of 1 trillion for the first year and 900 billion annually thereafter). When the cost of decontamination was added and revisions were made by the Cost Verification Committee, the minimum cost was calculated at 5.8 trillion yen. When this figure was divided by the electricity generated by the Fukushima nuclear power plant over a period of forty years, the committee estimated a 0.6 yen per kilowatt hour increase in the cost of electricity.

But what would the cost be in a worst-case scenario? Approximately 160,000 people were evacuated because of the nuclear accident in Fukushima. If the Tokyo metropolitan area were included in the evacuation area this would have meant the removal of 30 million people from Tokyo alone. With a simple calculation based on a comparison of the population of Tokyo and Fukushima, the cost of evacuating Tokyo would be two hundred times greater, and damages would be 1.2 quadrillion yen. The cost of nuclear power would rise to 120 yen per kilowatt-hour. Given that thermal power generation costs 12 yen per kilowatt-hour, one can see that nuclear power is exceedingly expensive.

At Fukushima, nuclear power's safety myth was destroyed and the myth of its cost-effectiveness along with it.

The Absence of Back-End Solutions

Naturally, after the accident at the Fukushima nuclear power plant, there has been a reconsideration of the cost of nuclear power even here in Japan. However, much of the discussion has emphasized the point that if we were to stop the operation of our nuclear power plants, the cost of natural gas and other fossil fuels would rise and electric companies would be forced to raise electricity prices. But if we continue to make use of nuclear power, we will produce nuclear waste containing plutonium, which is extremely dangerous and does not exist in nature.

We have not found any fundamental solutions with regard to what is referred to as the "back end," the intermediate storage of spent fuel, its reprocessing, and the treatment and disposal of radioactive waste. In the Japanese approach to the nuclear fuel cycle, the spent fuel from nuclear power plants is reprocessed to extract plutonium with the intention of using this plutonium to generate electricity in fast-breeder reactors. In this case, in addition to the plutonium used for fuel, additional plutonium is generated. With the hope that otherwise useless depleted uranium could be converted into plutonium, a large number of countries have attempted to develop fast-breeder reactors, but none have been able to make practical use of them. In Japan as well, when the sodium used as a coolant leaked out and caused an accident to occur at Monju's fast-breeder reactor in 1995, that operation was suspended. The technical problems and public concerns with fast-breeder reactors remain unsolved, and Japan's Monju facility is dormant.

Meanwhile, the spent fuel pools located adjacent to Japan's nuclear reactors are nearly full. I believe that if we reactivate our nuclear power plants, the electric companies would enjoy an improvement in the balance of payments, but there would be an increase in spent fuel and nuclear waste. When one considers the cost of treatment, the sooner we stop operating nuclear power plants, the better it will be for the national economy.

Plutonium has a half-life of 24,000 years, and for the toxicity of spent fuel to drop to the same level as natural uranium it takes at least 100,000 years. The operation and maintenance costs for that length of time are more than we can calculate. And even if we were to bury radioactive waste deep underground, we have no way of predicting crustal movement during that time.

Although the cost of nuclear-generated power is said to be less than thermal power, this only takes the cost incurred by the electric company into account, and only a small portion of the cost of treating the spent fuel is included in this calculation. Moreover, because the assumption is made that spent fuel will be reused, it is counted as a resource and placed on the books as an asset.

To promote nuclear power, the nuclear village says that spent fuel should be recycled, and to consume the plutonium thus generated, they say the development of fast-breeder reactors is necessary. Because fast-breeder reactors have failed to perform, they say that plutonium-thermal reactors are required, and they have introduced MOX fuels that are even more dangerous and more expensive to process. Promoting nuclear power as a justifiable cause, the nuclear village continues to invest huge sums of money, deviating far from sound economic principles.

The Problem of Electric Company Insolvency

The debate over whether to resume the operation of nuclear power plants has centered on (1) whether their safety has been adequately confirmed, and (2) whether there is enough electricity in the absence of nuclear power. But in fact, there is another major issue when determining whether or not to bring a plant back on line. If a plant is shut down and decommissioned, the electric company that owns it may become insolvent and go bankrupt. If a plant is operating, it is an asset, but if a nuclear reactor is decommissioned, it is of no value. This is to say that the financial health of the electric companies also has to be considered. I encounter those who speak with great emotion saying that electric companies should be dismantled or crushed, but nothing is solved by arguing at that level.

The matter of fiscal solvency is certainly of great importance to the electric companies, but it is important to the country as well.

When Japan Airlines (JAL), the national airline, failed, it continued steady operation while legal bankruptcy procedures such as debt consolidation and restructuring were handled one step at a time. In the context of reforms in electric power, electric companies that own nuclear power plants must find a way to avoid bankruptcy.

Immediately after the nuclear accident, there was a need for TEPCO, as the responsible party, to proceed with the work of containing the accident and compensating the victims. But when one considers the future of the nuclear power industry, in addition to the separation of electric power production from its distribution and transmission, TEPCO should consider separating nuclear power from its other work. Other electric companies, if they are not able to take full responsibility in the event of a nuclear accident, should also consider separating their nuclear divisions from their other endeavors. I hope that the management in Japan's electric companies will give serious thought to this.

The issue of whether or not to restart nuclear reactors is closely related to the financial health of the electric companies, a matter that needs to be understood by the general public as well. Therefore, when thinking about the future of nuclear power, in addition to a consideration of a nuclear power plant's safety, we must look at back-end costs and the financial health of the electric companies as well.

Renewing and Efficiently Using Energy

Japan's business world, showing some diffidence with regard to the electric industry, has not raised its voice in favor of the phasing out of nuclear power or the development of renewable energy, and yet the business climate has changed a little. Many companies have already entered the renewable energy field. When there is a potential for profits, businesses get serious. In fact, Japanese electrical manufacturers used to have state-of-the-art technology with respect to solar and wind energy generation. Because national policy favored nuclear power, these other technologies were not utilized. But in the future they will be. Japan has fallen far behind, but I believe we can rally.

The majority of investments in renewable energy will answer domestic demands and create new jobs. Moreover, unlike oil and natural gas, renewable energies do not have to be imported.

Energy conservation is a growth industry. While some people think energy conservation means foregoing the use of their air conditioner, they have it wrong. Though it is certainly good to consume less electricity, the use of products that consume less electricity is another form of energy conservation. The use of LED light bulbs is the classic example.

Some manufacturers have moved their factories overseas because of high domestic costs, but industries like the railroad have no choice but to do their business here at home. For this reason, railroad companies develop trains that run on less electricity, and I have heard that they have made great strides in this area. Department stores and convenience stores are making use of lighting, heating, air conditioning, and refrigeration units that consume less electricity.

Of course, many businesspeople understand these things, and in the business world, beneath the surface, there has been a tendency to move away from nuclear power and toward renewables. There are plans for wind generators floating off the coast of Fukushima Prefecture and the use of smart grids, and companies like Hitachi, Toshiba, and Mitsubishi Heavy Industries that have historically been central to the construction of nuclear power plants are participating.

If politicians push an energy policy that moves away from nuclear power and encourage technological development in renewables, energy conservation, and the use of cleaner fossil fuels, industries in these areas will enjoy even greater growth.

Dismantling the Nuclear Village

When one thinks rationally about back-end costs and so on, even before March 11 nuclear power had already reached a dead end, and it seems that the accident at the Fukushima nuclear power plant clarified that point for us. The decision to convert from nuclear power to renewable, natural energies is a matter of course. And yet for some reason we went so far as to build a pool adjacent to each reactor for the temporary storage of spent fuel. Why this fixation with nuclear power?

This is where the massive entourage of vested interests that make up the nuclear village comes in. On May 28, at the end of the first session of the National Diet of Japan Fukushima Nuclear Accident Independent Investigation Commission, I said the following:

> I believe the manner in which the military held sway over politics prior to the war and the actions of the nuclear village with the Federation of Electric Power Companies at its center have something in common. This is to say that over the past forty years, TEPCO and the Federation of Electric Power Companies have enjoyed a gradual tightening in their control over the administration of nuclear power. It is my understanding that their policy has been to ostracize and remove from the mainstream all experts, politicians, and bureaucrats who are critical of nuclear power. Further, to protect themselves, most who witnessed this ostracism looked on but offered no resistance. I say this with great remorse for I, too, am responsible.
>
> The nuclear village has yet to reflect seriously on the recent nuclear accident. If anything, they are attempting to gain a stronger

grip on the administration of nuclear power. To fundamentally reform the governance of nuclear power we must first elucidate the nuclear village's organizational and social psychological structures, which resemble those of the military before the war, and then dismantle them.

Prime Minister Noda's Energy Policy

After I resigned the position of prime minister, the administration of my successor, Yoshihiko Noda, gave its all to the comprehensive reform of social security and consumption tax. During that time, within the cabinet, METI Minister Edano, Minister of the Environment and Minister for the Restoration from and Prevention of Nuclear Accidents Hosono, and State Minister of National Strategy, Economic, and Fiscal Policy Furukawa led the way in establishing a new organization for the regulation of nuclear power, reviewing the Basic Energy Plan, addressing the resumption of the operation of nuclear power plants, and so on. Minister Hosono took the lead in promoting the establishment of the Nuclear Regulation Authority [NRA] to replace NISA. First, a bill was enacted to make the NRA a highly independent organization within the Ministry of the Environment, and then, after Prime Minister Noda appointed its members, the NRA was inaugurated, on September 19, 2012.

Beginning in October of the previous year, the Advisory Committee for Natural Resources and Energy, a deliberative body put together by METI, had been discussing the future of energy. Ultimately, the committee suggested three alternatives for the percentage of total electricity generated that should be generated by nuclear power in the year 2030: 0 percent, 15 percent, and 20–25 percent. The venue for consideration of this matter was then moved to the Energy and Environment Council of the National Policy Unit, which polled the general public with regard to the three alternatives. The result: a majority favored 0 percent.

During an ordinary session of the Diet, the Noda administration attempted the coordination of a strategy for innovative energy and the environment. In preparation for this, on August 24, within the Democratic Party, an Energy and Environment Research Committee was newly created with the policy chief Seiji Maehara as its chairman. I also became one of its advisers. Day after day, this was the site of heated debates.

I found that my many visits to sites and conversations with experts were helpful to my participation in these discussions. Bureaucrats say that electricity costs will rise if we phase out nuclear power generation. But I have visited the Rokkasho Nuclear Fuel Reprocessing Facility in Aomori and the Monju Nuclear Power Plant in Fukui. In addition to the matter of safety, the cost of operating these facilities and of disposing of radioactive waste is beyond measure, so I argued that such facilities have a negative impact on the economy as a whole. Ultimately, the Democratic Party's Energy and Environment Research Committee decided on a proposal to "invest all our policy resources in the realization of a nuclear-free Japan by the 2030s." The inclusion of a concrete deadline and of wording supporting the total elimination of nuclear energy was a great accomplishment. With a personal commitment to work for the achievement of freedom from nuclear power as early as 2025, I agreed with the committee's goals.

On September 14, consistent with the Democratic Party's conclusions, the Noda administration decided on a "strategy for innovative energy and the environment" as follows:

- An operational limit of forty years will be strictly applied to all nuclear power plants.

- Only those nuclear power plants that have been cleared by the Nuclear Regulation Authority can be restarted.
- On principle, no new nuclear power plants will be built and no additions will be made.

While applying the above three principles, all policy resources would be invested in the realization of a nuclear-free Japan by the 2030s. This policy matched the decisions that had been made by the Democratic Party.

Moving Away from Nuclear Power

In the midst of this process, prior to the summer of 2012, the decision was made to restart Kansai Electric's Oi Nuclear Power Plant. Related bureaucrats were unable to refute what were essentially METI's "electricity shortage" threats, and it came to pass that the plant reopening was announced at a press conference held by Prime Minister Noda. Within the Democratic Party as well, lively discussions continued among an energy project team chaired by Akihiro Ohata and a project team for the containment of nuclear accidents chaired by Satoshi Arai.

I felt that it was important, prior to a discussion of restarting individual nuclear power plants, to create a roadmap for a move away from the use of nuclear power. With that in mind, in April 2012 I created the Committee for the Consideration of a Roadmap for a Nonnuclear Japan with a membership of nearly seventy Democratic Party Diet members. In June, we proposed "the realization of a nuclear-free Japan by 2025." Around the same time, a group of citizens with whom I am acquainted who have lobbied widely for the end of nuclear power established the National Network for the Enactment of Legislation for the Phase-Out of Nuclear Power. The two groups cooperated to draw up a Fundamental Law for the

Phase-Out of Nuclear Power, which was submitted to the Diet on September 7, the last day of an ordinary session.

Every Friday in the summer of 2012, a large number of citizens gathered in front of the prime minister's compound to express their opposition to the restart of the Oi Nuclear Power Plant in Fukui. As a member of the ruling party and a former prime minister, I could never have imagined that this day would come. In fact, since the Fukushima disaster, there have been demonstrations and meetings all around the country. When I was young, student and citizens' movements were popular. There were a lot of rallies and meetings, but I sense a difference in the mood now. I am under the impression that recent citizens' movements are not like the left-wing antigovernment, antibusiness, or anti-American activism of the past. While they are political and social movements, they are also opportunities to transmit information and to express views.

These movements manifest the sentiment that "we no longer need nuclear power." Now, many citizens are expressing and discussing their doubts in their communities, workplaces, and families, and with friends. "We don't need nuclear power!" "But will we have enough electricity without it?" "Apparently there are renewable sources of energy." "Is nuclear power really cheap?" And so on.

The government's Energy and Environment Council held hearings throughout Japan, listening directly to the opinions of the people and gathering public comments by mail, facsimile, and e-mail as well. Many participated and shared their views, and it became clear that many Japanese wished for a nuclear-free Japan. The novelist Kenzaburo Oe also led the call for signatures on a "Goodbye to Nuclear Power Plants" petition, and by June 15, 751,000 signatures had been gathered. I was present in the Diet when the petition was presented and I could feel the excitement in the air.

The weekly Friday protests in front of the prime minister's compound were another expression of that passion. At one point I acted as a go-between, arranging for representatives of the demonstrators to meet with Prime Minister Noda. The prime minister listened thoroughly to what they had to say, and I believe he took it into consideration when making certain decisions that followed.

The Noda administration enacted an integrated tax and social security reform bill and disbanded the House of Representatives on November 16, 2012. In the general election that followed, the Democratic Party of Japan pledged a goal of "no nuclear power by the 2030s." While public opinion polls showed that approximately 70 percent of the people wanted a nuclear-free society, in the general elections voters showed strong disappointment with the highly factional Democratic Party. Furthermore, the antinuclear votes were split among other opposition parties, while the nuclear-tolerant Liberal Democratic Party took back a large number of parliamentary seats and enjoyed a major victory. However, the total number of people who voted for the Liberal Democrats was even less than in 2009 when they suffered a major defeat, clearly suggesting that the people were not actively endorsing the LDP's pronuclear policy.

In 2013, at the election for the House of Councillors as well, votes were split among the numerous parties that pledged a nuclear-free Japan, and as a result the LDP and Komeito, also tolerant of the use of nuclear energy, took enough seats to enjoy a majority in the House of Councillors.

When the Liberal Democratic Party regained power, Prime Minister Abe announced that he would wipe the slate clean with regard to the nuclear-free approach the Democratic Party had been pursuing. He would develop a new basic plan for Japan's energy.

Under the Noda cabinet the LDP had agreed to the founding of a new nuclear regulatory authority that was more independent than NISA and was taking a more cautious approach to the evaluation of nuclear power plants before restarting them. Then, in October 2013, Junichiro Koizumi, the former prime minister and a member of the LDP, spoke out in favor of a nonnuclear Japan. After visiting the spent-nuclear-fuel repository in Onkalo, Finland, Koizumi said that it was irresponsible to continue operating nuclear power plants. He began to call for an immediate end to the use of nuclear power, and the ripples started spreading through the LDP as well.

Decommissioning San Onofre

Since retiring from my position as prime minister, I have come to believe that it is my role to realize a nuclear-free Japan and a nuclear-free planet and to pursue an increase in new renewables. Toward that end I give talks in Japan and around the world, at the invitation of antinuclear groups.

I received an invitation from an antinuclear power citizens' group in California in June 2013. The San Onofre Nuclear Generating Station, which is located outside San Diego in Southern California, was shut down [in January 2012] because of radiation leaks. While the electric company showed an interest in restarting the plant, local citizens took action to stop it and asked me to share my experience as prime minister at the time of the Fukushima nuclear accident.

On the occasion of my visit, I was able to join a symposium with Gregory Jaczko, who served as chairman of the US Nuclear Regulatory Commission until July 2012; Peter Bradford, who was a member of the NRC at the time of the accident at Three Mile

Island; and Arnie Gunderson, a nuclear engineer who has called attention to problems inherent in nuclear power. I had the opportunity to exchange views with Mr. Jaczko prior to the symposium. Gregory Jaczko is a nuclear power expert who believes that it is impossible to completely guard against a nuclear accident. He also believes, I would learn, that one must consider how many people will be the victims of a nuclear accident should one occur, and that a nuclear power plant should not be built in a location such as Fukushima that requires the evacuation of a large number of people. I told him of the severity of the Fukushima nuclear accident, and of just how close we had come to evacuating an area with a radius of 250 kilometers and a population of 50 million people. Ultimately I came to realize that Mr. Jaczko and I were of the same mind.

Given the large number of people living in Los Angeles and San Diego, in the vicinity of the San Onofre Nuclear Generating Station, all in attendance listened intently to my story. Three days after the symposium, Southern California Edison, the owners of the San Onofre station, announced their decision to decommission the plant. In addition, they said that they would be pursuing the recovery of substantial damages from Mitsubishi Heavy Industries, which had supplied the plant with replacement steam generators that had been responsible for the radiation leaks.

The coalition of concerned citizens who had worked to stop operation of the plant was delighted by the owner's decision to decommission the plant, and they took out a full-page ad in the *Los Angeles Times* thanking those of us who had attended the symposium.

Thereafter, I was invited to participate in citizens' actions against Taiwan's Fourth Nuclear Power Plant, New York's Indian Point Energy Center, Boston's Pilgrim Nuclear Power Station, and so on. I have felt a pointed increase in antinuclear activism, not only in the United States and Asia, but in Europe as well.

Renewable Energy

Coincidentally, a bill for a feed-in tariff system was passed by my cabinet on the morning of the Fukushima nuclear accident. This bill was intended to promote the use of renewable energies through the establishment of a system whereby electricity generated by solar, wind, biomass, and other energies is bought at prices matched to the cost of the facilities required to generate them. In Europe and elsewhere, many countries had been doing this with good results for more than ten years, but in Japan, the nuclear village, led by the electric companies, had crushed such efforts.

Ultimately the opposition party agreed to see the cabinet's bill enacted in new energy legislation. The effect of this new system has been tremendous. In the year beginning July 2012, when the legislation went into effect, there were applications for the construction of solar power generation facilities with a capacity of 20 gigawatts, of which 3.5 gigawatts are already operational. In addition, plans are also under way for wind energy and biomass, and alternative energies are increasing at a rate such that we can anticipate renewable energy accounting for 20 percent of total energy generation on or around 2020. I can say with certainty that renewable energy will eventually provide more than 30 percent of Japan's energy, the share that nuclear power provided in its heyday.

I believe that in the future Japan will not need to make use of fossil fuels either and that we can meet all our energy needs from renewable sources. My hope is that this may one day be true throughout the world.

Acknowledgments

Working in my office in response to the nuclear accident, I was assisted by many people. The entire staff worked without a moment's rest, beginning with chief cabinet secretary Yukio Edano, METI's minister Banri Kaieda, deputy chief cabinet secretary Tetsuro Fukuyama, and my five special advisers: Koichi Kato, Goshi Hosono, Kiyomi Tsujimoto, Manabu Terada, and Hirokazu Shiba. In particular, the executive secretaries and counselors who were dispatched by each of the ministries to follow the condition of the reactors and spent fuel pools played an important role. I relied greatly on their information to respond promptly.

I would like to thank once again the executive secretaries for business affairs (Shiro Yamasaki, Shigeki Habuka, Keisuke Sadamori, Koichi Masuda, Tetsu Maeda, and Kanji Yamanouchi); the executive secretaries for political affairs (Kenji Okamoto, Jiro Hashimoto, Satoru Mizushima, Kaoru Hirakawa, Mitsuaki Kamata, Hiroki Toyooka, and Hiroshi Ikukawa); the executive secretaries (Seiji Ishida, Takuma Kajita, Yoshiaki Miyashita, Yuya Hasegawa, Futoshi Kohno, Takahiro Nagayama, and Keisuke Karaki); and others whose names I will not list here, including cabinet officials and security police.

I was also helped a great deal by the actions of cabinet secretary councilor Kenichi Shimomura, who was responsible for public relations; and by Yasushi Hibino, Masaki Saito, Masanori Aritomi, and Hiroshi Tasaka, whom I asked to advise me regarding the nuclear accident.

The team at the prime minister's office did their work well. To the extent that I was able to respond effectively to the nuclear accident, it was thanks to them. Among the executive secretaries and counselors, chief executive secretary Shiro Yamasaki was unfazed by my irritableness and he moved adroitly to keep the team together. And Kenji Okamoto remained at my side twenty-four hours a day as my point man for all communication.

With regard to my work after resigning from the post of prime minister, I have been helped a great deal in visiting renewable energy sites by Hiroaki Niihara, who worked for me as an executive secretary for business affairs prior to the nuclear accident. And I have enjoyed the support of Tamiyoshi Tachibana of the Society for the Study of Renewable Energy.

Many people collaborated with me in the publication of this book. Yusuke Nakagawa, a friend of many years, helped me with this book as he had with the book *Minister,* published by Iwanami Shinsho. I am also indebted to Yasuhiro Shigi and Hiroko Sohma of Gentosha, as my wife, Nobuko, was before me in the publication of her book.

And finally, I want to express my thanks to my wife, Nobuko, who, while handling activities in my home district, advises me with regard to the books and articles I should read.

I want to thank Jeffrey S. Irish for his translation. Given his intimate knowledge of Japanese culture and Japan's nuclear power problem, I am confident that he has rendered my prose in a manner that is at once true to my meaning and accessible to English-language readers. I am also most grateful to Mahinder Kingra and Susan Specter at Cornell University Press for taking on this project and helping me to share my experience and convictions with a wider world.

Acronyms

CNBC   Central Nuclear Biological Chemical Weapon Defense Unit

CRF   Central Readiness Force

IAEA   International Atomic Energy Agency

METI   Ministry of Economy, Trade, and Industry

MEXT   Ministry of Education, Culture, Sports, Science, and Technology

NAIIC   National Diet of Japan Fukushima Nuclear Accident Independent Investigation Commission

NISA   Nuclear and Industrial Safety Agency

NRA   Nuclear Regulation Authority

NSC   Nuclear Safety Commission

RCIC   reactor core isolation cooling system

SPEEDI   System for Prediction of Environmental Emergency Dose Information

Notes

Prologue

1. The following is an excerpt from "A Roughly Sketched Contingency Plan for Fukushima Daiichi Nuclear Power Plant" under the heading "The Accident as a Chain of Events" (p. 8).

1. A hydrogen explosion occurs in the core of or in the reactor containment vessel for reactor Unit 1, where the risk of such an occurrence is relatively high. Radioactive materials are released, and the flooding of Unit 1 is no longer possible. The reactor containment vessel is damaged.
2. Due to an increase in radiation, all workers are evacuated.
3. It becomes impossible to flood and cool reactor units 2 and 3 or the spent fuel rod pool located at Unit 4.
4. The fuel in the spent-fuel-rod pool located at Unit 4 is exposed and compromised, then melts. Thereafter, the molten fuel reacts with the concrete, and radioactive materials are released. (The following pages show an increase in the damage to the spent-fuel-rod pool.)

The document also presents the following discussion regarding estimated radiation levels (p. 15):

Thereafter, the spent fuel rods in the pools located in the other reactor buildings will also be compromised, and a reaction of the molten fuel with the concrete will result in the release of large quantities of radioactive material. As a result, there is a possibility that a forced evacuation will be required for an area as great as 170 kilometers [106 miles], and that annual radiation levels will far exceed natural levels in an area possibly extending to 250 kilometers [155 miles], whereby those requesting evacuation from this area would have to be recognized.

"With the passage of time, the area requiring evacuation will be reduced in size, but given a natural attenuation of radiation levels, it will take several dozen years for this to occur within an area of 170 and 250 kilometers [106 and 155 miles].

2. While the present-day Japanese legal system does not prescribe martial law, the Civil Protection Law (legislation for measures to be taken to protect the public in the event of an armed attack and the like) gives the prime minister a great deal of authority. However, because this law is intended to cope with a military attack or a major act of terrorism, it is difficult to apply it to a nuclear accident. The prime minister can declare a state of emergency in keeping with article 71 of the Police Act. "In the event of a large-scale disaster, riot, or other emergency situation, and when it is deemed necessary to the maintenance of the public order, the prime minister may, with the counsel of the National Public Safety Commission, declare a state of emergency either nationwide or in a particular area." Also, article 105 of the Basic Act on Disaster Control Measures, stipulates that "when an extreme natural accident occurs, and when said disaster has a dramatic effect on the nation's economy and the public's welfare, and when it is extraordinary and severe, if it is recognized that there is a particular need for the promotion of emergency measures for the handling of said disaster, the prime minister may, after submitting the matter to the cabinet, declare a state of emergency in all related areas or in one particular area." However, this does not concretely specify the legal powers the prime minister has over the people.

Meanwhile, the Act on Special Measures concerning Countermeasures for Large-Scale Earthquakes is designed for the issuance of a warning regarding a potential earthquake, and to give evacuation orders and the like. It does not provide for flight from radiation in the event of a nuclear accident. In the past, taking into account the possibility of a large-scale natural disaster, an invasion from abroad, a terrorist act, rioting, and other such emergencies, there was a move to create basic legislation for the handling of emergency situations. In 2004, the Democratic Party of Japan, the Liberal Democratic Party of Japan, and Komeito reached such an agreement, though many voices were raised against the idea for fear of the possibility that fundamental freedoms protected by the constitution, including property rights, would be drastically limited, and no legislation was passed.

3. From Gorbachev's *Memoirs*, translated by Georges Peronansky and Tatjana Varsavsky, published by Doubleday, 1996.

1. Memories from the Abyss

1. Later, after this had been pointed out to me, I asked a lawyer to confirm this matter. When I learned that the donor was a Korean national born in Japan and that they still had Korean citizenship, I returned the donated money. An

accusation was made to the Tokyo District Public Prosecutors Office but was rejected. There had been a further petition to the committee for the inquest of prosecutions, but it was concluded that it was not an indictable offense, meaning that the matter had been brought to an end in legal terms.

2. In fact, this was the first time that an Emergency Disaster Response Headquarters had been established. Article 24 of the Basic Act on Disaster Control Measures states that "in the event of an extraordinary disaster, in keeping with the scale and other aspects of said disaster, when it is determined that there is a special need to take emergency measures" the prime minister "may establish a provisional extraordinary disaster response headquarters at the cabinet office." However, in this case, we determined that the earthquake surpassed the scale of an "extraordinary disaster," and was in keeping with article 28.2 of the same act, which states that "in the event of a particularly remarkable and devastating disaster, when it is determined that there is a special need to take emergency measures," an Emergency Disaster Response Headquarters can be established. The Emergency Disaster Response Headquarters' administrative staff is appointed by the prime minister from among the cabinet secretariat, the staff of designated administrative agencies, and the heads or members of the staff of designated local administrative agencies.

3. The first wave of the tsunami struck the Fukushima Daiichi Nuclear Power Plant at 3:27 p.m., and it is thought that the second wave arrived [eight minutes later,] at 3:35. As a result, reactor units 1 through 5 at Fukushima Daiichi all suffered from a total loss of electricity, a station blackout. In addition, reactor units 1, 2, and 4 lost all direct current [DC] power. At 3:42 p.m. TEPCO reported to METI's Nuclear and Industrial Safety Agency [NISA] that the specific events defined in article 10 of the Nuclear Emergency Preparedness Act had occurred. Then, approximately one hour later, at 4:45 p.m., in keeping with the occurrence of the specific events defined in article 15, TEPCO reported to NISA their failure to flood and thereby cool the reactor cores of reactor units 1 and 2. Article 10 of the Nuclear Emergency Preparedness Act also states that when an accident occurs, "if radiation levels in the vicinity of the nuclear power plant are detected in excess of the standard levels specified by government decree," all related ministers, local governors, and local mayors must be informed.

This is to say that in keeping with article 10, when a specific event occurs with regard to a nuclear power plant, it is reported to the relevant minister, and if it is deemed to reflect an emergency state, the minister will inform the prime minister. Following this procedure, Minister Kaieda reported to me, and, as per article 15.2, I immediately issued an official announcement of a nuclear emergency.

4. In article 20 of the Nuclear Emergency Preparedness Act, the director-general of the Nuclear Emergency Response Headquarters (the prime minister) is given the authority, when it is deemed necessary to the quick and unerring execution of an emergency response in the area designated as the

emergency-response-measures implementation area, to act within the bounds deemed necessary and may give the necessary instructions to the heads of designated national and regional government organizations, and, in keeping with the regulations in the previous article, to the heads and administrative staff of designated national and regional government organizations and other administrative organizations, designated national and regional public organizations, and the operators of nuclear power plants.

5. J-Village is a national soccer training center. The facilities were originally built by TEPCO and donated to Fukushima Prefecture. Immediately after the earthquake disaster, as the facilities had not suffered major damage, they were used as an evacuation area. However, because it was within a twenty-kilometer radius of Fukushima's Daiichi Nuclear Power Plant, as of March 12 it could no longer be used as a shelter. On the fifteenth, it was transferred to the jurisdiction of the national government and was used by the Japan Ground Self-Defense Forces' helicopters and personnel as a drop-off location for the decontamination of radioactive materials. Then, beginning on March 18, it became an on-site coordination point for the government, TEPCO, the Japan Ground Self-Defense Forces, and the police and fire departments in their efforts to respond to the nuclear accident. I visited J-Village on April 2, and again on July 16.

6. Tokyo is so large and heavily populated it is on equal footing with Japan's prefectures and has a governor instead of a mayor.

2. Taking Action before Stepping Down

1. In August and again in October 2015 a total of two nuclear reactors in Kagoshima Prefecture, in southwest Kyushu, were reactivated.

About the Author

Naoto Kan

Born in Ube City, Yamaguchi Prefecture in 1946. Ninety-fourth prime minister of Japan. Held office for 452 days, from June 2010 to September 2011. Graduated Tokyo Institute of Technology's Faculty of Science in 1970. Presently residing in Musashino, Tokyo, and serving his tenth term in the House of Representatives. Also a patent lawyer. First elected in 1980 as deputy head of the Socialist Democratic Federation. After acting as policy chief of the New Party Sakigake, served as minister of health and welfare in Prime Minister Hashimoto's first cabinet, January to November 1996. Created the Democratic Party of Japan the same year and became its leader. Became leader, policy chief, and chief secretary of newly reformed Democratic Party of Japan in 1998. Served as deputy prime minister, minister of state for national policy, and minister of finance under Prime Minister Hatoyama. Presently top adviser to the Democratic Party of Japan. Publications include *Minister* (Iwanami Shinsho). This is Kan's first book to be translated into English. It has been translated into German as well.

About the Translator

Jeffrey S. Irish

Writer, translator, and associate professor with extensive experience in rural Japan. Twice mayor of a mountain village in southwestern Japan, population thirty. Studied Japanese history as an undergraduate at Yale University and Japanese folk culture as a graduate student at Harvard University. Has written five books in Japanese about rural Japan, translated three books from Japanese into English, and for nine years was a columnist for the *South Japan Times*. Translation of Miyamoto Tsuneichi's classic *The Forgotten Japanese* was published in 2010 by Stone Bridge Press. Also translates subtitles for Japanese documentary films with a specialization in environmental and cultural matters. Teaches courses in community regeneration at the International University of Kagoshima and lives in a small farming community with his wife and two children.